PRACTICAL THEOLOGY
in **CHURCH** and **SOCIETY**

PRACTICAL THEOLOGY
in CHURCH and SOCIETY

Joseph E. Bush Jr.

CASCADE Books • Eugene, Oregon

PRACTICAL THEOLOGY IN CHURCH AND SOCIETY

Copyright © 2016 Joseph E. Bush Jr. All rights reserved. Except for brief quotations in critical publications or reviews, no part of this book may be reproduced in any manner without prior written permission from the publisher. Write: Permissions, Wipf and Stock Publishers, 199 W. 8th Ave., Suite 3, Eugene, OR 97401.

Cascade Books
An Imprint of Wipf and Stock Publishers
199 W. 8th Ave., Suite 3
Eugene, OR 97401

www.wipfandstock.com

PAPERBACK ISBN 13: 978-1-4982-8274-1
HARDCOVER ISBN 13: 978-1-4982-8276-5
EBOOK ISBN: 978-1-4982-8275-8

Cataloguing-in-Publication data:

Name: Bush, Joseph Earl, 1956–.

Title: Practical theology in church and society / Joseph E. Bush Jr.

Description: Eugene, OR: Cascade Books, 2016 | Includes bibliographical references and index.

Identifiers: ISBN: 978-1-4982-8274-1 (paperback) | ISBN: 978-1-4982-8276-5 (hardback) | 978-1-4982-8275-8 (ebook)

Subjects: Theology—Practical. | Church and the world. | Liberation theology. | Organizational behavior. | Title.

Classification: BV3 B80 2016 (print) | BV3 (ebook)

Manufactured in the U.S.A.   07/15/16

Scripture quotations taken from the New American Standard Bible®, Copyright © 1960, 1962, 1963, 1968, 1971, 1972, 1973, 1975, 1977, 1995 by The Lockman Foundation. Used by permission. (www.Lockman.org).

Figure 23 is from Joe Holland and Peter Henriot, SJ, *Social Analysis* (1983), and is used with permission. "Pastoral Circle" and "Center of Concern" are trademarks of Center of Concern (www.coc.org).

Dedicated to my father and mother:
Joseph E. Bush Sr. and Virginia Curtis Bush

Contents

Introduction to the Book and Its Author | ix

Part 1: Reflection on Practice
1 Action and Reflection | 3
2 Entering a Congregation's Culture | 16
3 Liminal Leadership | 29
4 Reflective Practitioners | 51
5 Framing and Reframing Congregations as Organizations | 69

Part 2: Methodological Movements
6 Theology in Church and Society | 93
7 A Constructive Approach | 104
8 Liberation Theology | 124
9 Practical Theology | 135
10 Solidarity and Suspicion | 146
11 Reflexivity: Looking Back, Looking Ahead | 157

Bibliography | 175
Index | 181

Introduction to the Book and Its Author

THIS IS A BOOK about reflection on ministry. It grows out of my own experience in ministry as well as my work in the seminary classroom where students and I have been able to discuss our respective experiences together. This book is written not only with these students in mind but also our many colleagues of every denomination who are already productively engaged in ministry.

One experience common to all of us is the challenge we face when we enter a new situation of ministry—when we become involved with a new congregation or agency located in a new neighborhood or community with its own history and network of relationships. This is a challenge faced by seminarians who find themselves serving ministry internships while they are engaged in theological field education. Later we experience this challenge again as we are called or appointed to our first parish or other ministering situation after graduation. It is also a challenge that recurs for us throughout our ministering career whenever we move into new situations of ministry.

Many readers, especially those who are currently facing such a challenge of entry to a new place of ministry, may want to skip the rest of this introduction for now and turn directly to chapter 1. The first few chapters address this challenge of beginning ministry in a new place with new people. Each chapter introduces a few strands of theory and then focuses attention on specific cases for reflection. The context of entering a new situation of ministry is assumed for the first half of the book. Readers can simply start in chapter 1 and read until desiring a wider theoretical introduction to the book as a whole. At that point, readers might then return to this introduction for the desired overview.

This book begins in simplicity and builds in complexity. We wade gradually into deeper waters, finding that we can swim. The book as a whole

Introduction to the Book and Its Author

is really about method for theological reflection as we engage in ministry. It is not a handbook on starting ministry or on doing ministry per se, but on deepening our understanding about our own ministerial practice and that of our congregations as we engage the wider social community.

In many ways, this book on the subject of practical theology now picks up where my first book, *Gentle Shepherding*,[1] left off, though that continuity may not be immediately obvious to readers acquainted with that earlier work. *Gentle Shepherding* grew out of experiences with seminarians studying professional ethics for church leaders. I have been gratified by that book's reception and its continued use as a textbook in seminary classrooms. Its focus is primarily on decision-making ethics for clergy. It places pastoral ethics within the larger conversation about professional ethics and draws on ethical theory from Western philosophical traditions. It does so always with the broad range of pastoral duties in mind—whether pastoral care or church mission or leadership and administration. The focus, though, is always on ethics; it does not attempt to provide a broader methodological framework for reflecting on ministry more generally beyond the task of discerning moral responsibility in the practice of ministry. *Gentle Shepherding* concludes by glimpsing the broader vocational landscape of both the church's evangelical calling and the calling of all humanity to strive for justice, peace, and ecological flourishing. It concludes there however.

This book on practical theology now does provide that broader method for reflection on practice that *Gentle Shepherding* does not. It provides that method while attending to our practice as individuals in ministry, to our corporate practice as congregations in ministry, and to our practice as Christians within the larger society.

The cyclical method provided here is not new. As we will see, there have been many iterations of this basic methodology over the last several decades—with different emphases, priorities, nuances, and nomenclature. In fact, there have been so many iterations of it that it becomes potentially confusing for theological students being introduced to these various versions in different contexts of study. I hope to show in this book, however, that this basic method is quite elegant in its simplicity even while it is inspiring of a plurality of expression. My aim here is not to unite these expressive voices to sing in unison, but rather to bring them adjacent to one another into something like a chorus so that both their harmony and their points of discord can be appreciated.

---

1. Bush, *Gentle Shepherding*.

Introduction to the Book and Its Author

Several areas of theological study are brought into conversation here. Liberation theology, missiology, contextual studies, congregational studies, practical theology, Christian social ethics, and theological field education name some of them. All can be seen to share something of a methodological similarity in relation to each other even as they define distinct areas of discourse. It is my hope that this book can provide a resource for students and ministers engaged in any of these areas of reflection. It can be read in association with the literature in each of these areas in order to provide an integrative perspective that might help readers to link between them. For those who have already been engaged in the practice of ministry for several years, I further hope that this book can help link the areas of instruction during one's years in seminary and the ongoing development of theological disciplines as reflected in the current literature.

My own journey with this material begins with my experience as a student at Wesley Theological Seminary in the early 1980s and extends to my current practice as the Director of the Practice in Ministry and Mission at my alma mater. It was in seminary that I was exposed to liberation theology and to the hermeneutical circle of Juan Luis Segundo.[2] The need to ground theological reflection in actual experience was impressed upon me. In particular, our experience of social contradictions and human suffering, I began to realize, could and should inform a critical suspicion of both ideology and theology.

As I left seminary and entered ministry in the postindustrial city of Paterson, New Jersey, I found that this put me in good stead to attend appreciatively to my parishioners and to their experiences, especially their experiences of poverty and vulnerability. As a man of middle-class background and economic privilege, I needed such a method to urge me across the divides of economic class, gender, and culture in order to be in more authentic fellowship with those I was called to serve.

When later I entered graduate school at Drew University in the area of Religion and Society, I was able to explore further some of the theoretical underpinnings of this methodology. I was especially attentive to its earlier German roots in the sociology and social ethics of Max Weber and Ernst Troeltsch[3] and to the more recent American model provided by the

---

2. Segundo, *Liberation of Theology*, 9.

3. My reading of Troeltsch's *Social Teaching of the Churches* in particular alerted me to notice the continuing dialectical relationship between the social forces at work shaping ideology and the church's life and witness in society at any given time and place. This has in turn informed my understanding of the cyclical methodologies described in this

constructive work of James Cone. It was also in graduate school at Drew that I became increasingly aware of other ways of culturally contextualizing theology and ministry, and I was especially drawn to the work of Robert Schreiter in *Constructing Local Theologies*.[4]

This attention to culture as the context for theology prepared me better than I realized at the time for my first full-time teaching appointment at the Pacific Theological College (PTC) in the Republic of Fiji. The keystone of PTC's curriculum was missiological concern and the contextualization of theology to South Pacific cultures. The student body and the faculty were from nations throughout Oceania and the world: Marshall Islands, Kiribati, Tuvalu, Nauru, Samoa, American Samoa, Tonga, French Polynesia, Niue, New Caledonia, Vanuatu, Solomon Islands, Papua New Guinea, Australia, New Zealand, Germany, Mauritius, Canada, England, India, Indonesia, the USA, and Fiji and Rotuma. No ethnic group was in a majority. My primary area of instruction was Church and Society, but I taught broadly in the area of Church Ministries.

In this multicultural context marked by the challenges of decolonization and nation building, I found both Robert Schreiter's work on local theologies and the methods of liberation theologies to provide helpful resources. In particular, I found the liberationist method of the Pastoral Circle as articulated by Joe Holland and Peter Henriot in their book *Social Analysis* to be extremely helpful in its simplicity and accessibility. I find it still is, and it features prominently in the pages that follow.[5]

Following my years in Fiji, I joined the faculty of the School of Ministry for the Presbyterian Church of Aotearoa New Zealand, teaching in the area of the Ministry of the Whole People of God in Church and Society. Theological field education was the keystone of this two-year program for ordinands. Students served in ministry internships during the entire time and met concurrently in field education seminars to reflect on their experiences together. Methods for theological reflection on situations of ministry became part of our daily diet in these seminars. In this context, I was drawn to writers in the British Commonwealth—Denham Grierson in Australia

---

book. My appreciation for Troeltsch deepened though conversations with Thomas W. Ogletree; see his *World Calling*.

4. Schreiter, *Constructing Local Theologies*.

5. Holland and Henriot, *Social Analysis*. "Pastoral Circle" and "Center of Concern" are trademarks of Center of Concern (www.coc.org).

Introduction to the Book and Its Author

and especially to Laurie Green in the UK.[6] A strength of Green's method is its intuitive nature. Especially in theological field education, where students can sometimes be baffled by the complexity of actual situations and where emotional investment in the situation might be quite high, simplicity of method is a virtue. In these reflective moments, the most erudite method might actually be distracting to participants. It needs to work for students in the heat of the teachable moment. Green's methodology, while being deeply informed theoretically, has this quality. It also features prominently in the pages that follow. Green continues to revise his method to make it ever more accessible.

I have continued to work in theological field education since returning to the United States, initially at United Theological Seminary of the Twin Cities and currently at Wesley Theological Seminary. At United, we linked field education with coursework in leadership, organization, and administration and finance. Congregational studies and organizational theory have informed my pedagogy and have guided my own reflections with students. A standard textbook in congregational studies has been and still is *Studying Congregations: A New Handbook.*[7] Three aspects of this *Handbook* I find to be of continuing help to students in reflecting on their own experiences in congregational ministry. The first is Jackson Carroll's chapter on reflective practice and leadership. The second is the basic method of reframing that informs the overall approach of the *Handbook*. The third is Robert Schreiter's chapter on practical theology. In each instance, the *Handbook* provides a helpful introduction to the material, which I find benefits from further explanation, elaboration, and conversation. I dialog with this material from the *Handbook* in the pages that follow. Chapter 4 introduces reflective practice and leadership with reference to Anita Farber-Robertson's interpretation of the work of Donald Schön and Chris Argyris.[8] Chapters 4 and 5 introduce methods of reframing generally, and elaborate on the roots of this method in organizational theory specifically. Chapter 9 draws from Schreiter's chapter as a point of departure for comparing various methodological approaches to practical theology.

At Wesley Theological Seminary, I currently teach a course on "Practical Theology in Church and Society," and I lecture on "Practical Theology

---

6. Grierson, *Transforming a People of God*; Green, *Let's Do Theology*.

7. Ammerman et al., eds., *Studying Congregations*.

8. Farber-Robertson, *Learning While Leading*; see also Argyris and Schön, *Theory in Practice*.

Introduction to the Book and Its Author

for Urban Ministry" for our program in urban ministry. This book has been most immediately nurtured in the contexts of these courses and in the conversations with students in these courses. Practical theologians that we have been reading and discussing include Thomas Groome, Don Browning, Richard Osmer, Pamela Couture, and Dale Andrews. These individuals are profound thinkers and prolific authors. I am content to be in conversation with them. This book does not stand alone; it is a part of a larger conversation. It is my hope that readers of this book will be reading these practical theologians as well. This book can serve as an introduction to the subject of practical theology but not as a comprehensive guide. It is my hope that many readers will want to read the works of these authors and to benefit from the depth of their contributions to the field.

These are the strands that are woven together into the fabric of this book. The book proceeds in two parts. As already mentioned, it starts in simplicity and grows in complexity. Part 1 moves incrementally and sequentially into different moments or aspects of reflection on practice. While I hope that all engaged in ministry will find this material speaking to their situation, I think that the tools introduced in the chapters of part 1 will be particularly helpful to students in missiology, congregational studies, or theological field education. This material in part 1 is rooted in the practice of ministry. Part 1 alone might be sufficient for many readers. Each chapter of this book—whether in part 1 or part 2—includes exercises for reflection that keep our thinking grounded.

Part 2 starts to make the methodological connections with greater intentionality and greater detail. It is in part 2 of this book that the various moments and methods of theological reflection on practice as introduced above are critically compared to each other. Part 2 is a movement toward greater integration of the various theological and methodological components introduced here. It will provide greater methodological detail for readers whose interest has been piqued, perhaps readers engaged in courses on practical theology or systematic theology. Both part 1 and part 2 of this book pertain to both theory and practice, but in part 2 the theory comes more to the fore as the method is made increasingly explicit.

Finally, I want to conclude this Introduction by noticing the obvious. Ministry always has a social context. To reflect on practice is not just an individual endeavor. Nor can it be simply confined to congregations. Our ministry in congregations is at once informed by and engaged with the larger social world of which we are a part. This book begins by

Introduction to the Book and Its Author

affirming the importance of social context for ministry and for our individual social locations. It then moves to consider in order of an increasingly widening community of interest: reflection on individual action, reflection on congregational practices, and finally reflection taking into account those powerful social forces that define the larger social praxis of the church's ministry.

I want to thank the students in my classes, internships, and intercultural immersions at Wesley Theological Seminary, United Theological Seminary of the Twin Cities, the Presbyterian School of Ministry in New Zealand, and the Pacific Theological College in Fiji. All have taught me. At United Theological Seminary of the Twin Cities, I benefited greatly from conversations with my fellow team-teachers, Eleazar Fernandez and Sharon Tan, for the course "Integration of Ministry and Local Theologies."

I want to give special thanks to the 2014 class in "Practical Theology in Church and Society" at Wesley Seminary, who read the manuscript for this book and participated with me in the exercises for reflection. I have much gratitude to Wesley Seminary for providing sabbatical time. I am especially grateful to my colleagues in the Practice of Ministry and Mission (PMM) office, Josie Hoover, Desirée Barnes, Joe Tortorici, Youtha Hardman-Cromwell, Kate D'Alessandro, and all of the PMM colloquy leaders who have covered for me in my absence. Kate D'Alessandro helped greatly with proofreading and editing some of this material. Also my wife, Elizabeth, includes among her many talents a keen editor's eye and a sharp pencil.

I am deeply grateful to Rev. Bob Maddox and the Briggs Center for Faith and Action for providing me with a sabbatical office in the Carpenter House. Bob is inspiring in his humble perseverance in faithful witness for a more just society—whether serving as an advisor to the president of the United States or making peanut butter sandwiches for distribution to the hungry through Martha's Table. Thanks, all.

PART 1

Reflection on Practice

1

Action and Reflection

Practice and Action

THE TITLE OF THIS book suggests two areas of tension, each of which represents a dialectical relationship. One of these is the relationship between church and society. This refers to the relationship between church as the community of faith and the wider society of which the church is a part. Society is the larger community or communities encompassing the faithful, surrounding the faithful, from which the faithful come, to which the faithful go, and in which the faithful live. Society is organized in different ways and can be viewed through different lenses: ecological relationships, political relationships, cultural relationships, and the various social institutions within which people find themselves related.

The other tension, or dialectical relationship, is implied in the very phrase, "practical theology." To some, this sounds like an oxymoron. Theology is about matters of ultimacy and even of ultimate mystery. This is implied in the etymological meaning of *theology*, which is a "word about God" or the study of God. In contrast, the *practical* is about the more proximate—what we do in the here and now. It refers to that which is accessible to human experience in a rather direct way. At the same time, though, practical experience can have profound implications. We realize that "what we do" has a lot to do with "who we are." There are deep, mysterious, and even ultimate questions that are raised as we interact with one another in society. The way we are in the world here and now is of theological concern.

Part 1: Reflection on Practice

Practical theology places the question in the concrete, so that we reflect theologically on actual experience and practice. This is the second dialectic—the relationship between reflection and practice—between thought and experience—between our ideas and the realities of our existence as we perceive them.

To reflect on practice is to engage in praxis. *Praxis* is the Greek word meaning "practice." In contemporary theology and educational theory, praxis refers to the process of reflection itself which attends to practice. It refers to any method that allows us to reflect critically or analytically on practice. Such a method is praxeological. Practical theology is a praxeological way of approaching theology. It brings theological reflection into critical dialogue with our practice.

While practice serves to ground theology concretely in the experienced here and now, the idea of practice itself covers much ground. Seemingly a simple idea at first, the concept of "practice" proves to be very complex upon reflection. In particular, it indicates several different dimensions of human experience. It can refer to the personal experiences and actions of an individual, on one hand. On the other hand, it can refer to the vast political, economic, and social systems that shape and constrain individual action.

The scale might be local or global. The focus might be broad through the wide-angle lens of social systems, or it might narrow to the actions and experiences of an individual. The narrowing and widening of focus and scale indicate some of the complexity in the idea of practice and suggest the importance of such corollary dialectical comparisons as global/local and personal/social.

It can be clarifying at times to distinguish more sharply between different levels, foci, scope, or types of practice. Such distinctions can be helpful for reflecting more precisely on different aspects of human experience, but they should not be rigidly overdrawn. This and subsequent chapters focus attention on some of these different dimensions of practice. These chapters expand in scope sequentially from a narrower focus on personal action to a broader scope on professional practice and on congregational ministry to a very broad scope on social realities and globalizing social forces. It will be seen nonetheless that the broader social context is unavoidably present even in personal decisions and actions.

Thomas W. Ogletree, a Christian ethicist, distinguishes between action and practice while noticing that the two ideas are very much related to each other and are often used synonymously. Ogletree suggests the idea of "practice" tends to refer to more routinized patterns of acting, and "action" tends to refer to more individualized occurrences. He explains:

> Practice suggests the repetition, even routinization, of particular patterns of acting, perhaps until they are virtually 'second nature.' Action may refer to a unique response or initiative within a particular situation. Action in this latter sense requires fresh deliberation and judgment about what is to be done.[1]

Ogletree continues by noting that Christian ethicists often concentrate their attention on the morality of particular actions with an interest in justifying particular decisions. Yet, at the same time, he observes that the ideas of action and practice can be largely interchangeable. He writes that action can refer both to "unique actions and routinized patterns of social practice." Indeed, according to Ogletree, Christian social ethics looks beyond individual actions to examine the larger "social context and forms of human action."[2]

Let us look, therefore, at these increasingly complex levels of practice, recognizing that even the most individualized actions are never entirely isolated but occur within a wider social context. The remainder of this chapter will examine particular actions and decisions and notice the ways in which social context informs them. Subsequent chapters will turn to the idea of professional practice as a set of expectations for certain individuals. These expectations pertain to the establishing of a professional's routines and conduct over time. A particular focus in the following chapters will be on the profession of the clergy.

More broadly, though, we will also attend to the idea of a congregation's practice within its community—both the parish as local neighborhood and the wider understanding of both parish and neighbor. We will examine the idea of social practice with reference to broader social institutions, cultural patterns, and forms of social power. This broader social dimension is a complex but important area of practice, and this book will further equip readers with tools for analysis of social praxis in the service of ministry.

---

1. Ogletree, *World Calling*, 49.
2. Ibid.

PART 1: REFLECTION ON PRACTICE

Action in Community

An individual's action always occurs within social patterns that give meaning to that action—that ascribe importance and moral value to the action. To reflect on an action within these frames of moral value and social meaning is to engage in ethical analysis of the action. Ethics, in this regard, might be understood as a branch of practical theology. The aim is to bring theological meaning and moral clarity to the action or decision being contemplated.

Decision-making ethics may focus on an individual's particular decision but with an eye to the social expectations of a community, the community's moral norms, and a weighing of the consequences to members of that community. Sometimes the community in question is simply assumed, but the community itself is never absent. Writers in ethics often describe aspects of the community as the social context for the problem being addressed, or they may clarify the social location of their own analysis. In situations involving decision-making ethics, there may be several such aspects of community: (1) the social context of the decision itself, (2) the social location of the individuals involved in that decision; (3) the community of moral discourse informing the writer's or observer's argument, and (4) the writer's or observer's own social location. The first two of these aspects of community shall each be further clarified below.

Social Context of Decisions and Actions

Since so much of contemporary social life is organized within institutions, the social context of the decision itself is often identified as a kind of institution. For instance, a medical decision might be taking place within a hospital setting. A business decision might be taking place within a corporate setting. A decision about ministry might be taking place within a congregation and its surrounding parish. A legal decision would be taking place within a courtroom but pertain to a context beyond that courtroom.

Matters of policy are broader than questions about specific decisions, but policies are also determined within institutional frameworks: e.g. structures of government for shaping public policy or denominational judicatories for ecclesial policies. In fact such broader policies in turn provide part of the influential context for specific decisions. Broader institutional policies guide specific decisions and are, in turn, based upon historical patterns of specific decisions and the kinds of problems encountered.[3] Besides the institutional context, however, there are other important dimensions of the social context for a particular decision. The country, culture, and economic conditions surrounding the decision are also critical. This leads to the second aspect of community that is important in any particular decision: the social location of the individuals themselves who may be involved in that decision.

Social Location of Individuals

In any one individual's decision about a course of action, there may be myriad other individuals involved at different levels. One way to think about the involvement of various people in the action of a single individual is to think about their grammatical relationship to each other with regard to the action in question. Who is acting toward whom? An action is a verb. Who is the subject of that action? That is, whose action is it? The person who is the subject of the action is the moral "agent." In addition to the moral agent, one might also ask, who are the other individuals involved who might be the grammatical objects or recipients of that action? These all may be said to have social location.

Subjects of Action

In ethical discourse, the person who acts is often called the "agent." A person's power to act in a situation is his or her "agency." In legal discourse, however, an agent acts on behalf of another, who is called the "principal," and to whom the agent is obliged. In any contemplated action, is the decision-maker acting autonomously or is this action being done on behalf of another or others? In pastoral ethics, this can be a very lively question. When is a pastor acting on his or her own and therefore acting purely out of his or her own inner conscience, and when is that pastor acting on behalf of others and constrained/empowered by expectations of others and a constellation of consciences?

The social location of the person acting as a moral agent is always important for understanding that person's agency. If a person has been empowered to act, we might ask how this person has been so empowered and

---

3. Dyck, *On Human Care*, 19–21, 34.

by whom. Sometimes, that power has been clearly and explicitly delimited, as in a relationship between employer and employee or in that between a professional and a client. The client empowers the professional to act in the client's best interests. The employer empowers the employee to act in a way consistent with the responsibilities of that person's job. A pastor is empowered by a congregation to function in certain capacities but not in others. These relationships are all formally established, which helps to clarify the power to act of the respective parties.

At other times, though, a person's agency or power to act is more tacitly assumed. Society empowers some more than others. We expect some to exercise leadership, but we are suspect of others. These expectations fall into patterns that divide society into the more powerful and the less powerful. These divisions persist over time in ways that prove frustrating for those whose voice and whose power have been diminished historically. Racism, classism, sexism, and heterosexism all play into this dynamic. Indeed, these patterns of social division and selective empowerment can be internalized by a person over time so that subordinate status becomes a part of that person's self-image. Thus, even when the formal structures might change to permit and even welcome a wider participation from those who have been marginalized historically, those persons still may not feel empowered.

Recipients of Action

In addition to the agents who are the subjects of a contemplated action, who are the grammatical "objects" or recipients of that action? That is, who is being affected by the actions of an agent? There may be a particular individual who is the intended recipient of a person's care and the focus of that person's attention. G. J. Warnock referred to this person as the "moral patient"—one who is the recipient of the moral agent's actions.[4] Mutual understanding can be facilitated when the moral agent and the moral patient share a social context and a similar worldview. Such commonality allows for a kindness to be interpreted as a kindness, for a harm to be fully appreciated as a harm, or for justice to be recognized as justice. When there is not a shared cultural context, then different values and expectations can

---

4. Warnock, *Object of Morality*, 148, cited by Frankena, "Ethics and the Environment," 5; see also Loetscher, "Use of a Distinction between Moral Agent, Moral Patient and Object," who distinguishes further between moral patients, who have a stake in moral actions, and mere objects, which do not.

frustrate people's attempts to honor one another (though genuine goodwill can do a lot to transcend cultural confusion and to assuage resultant faux pas). A shared culture allows for a shared world of meaning and a greater affinity of values.

Moreover, a shared social location within that culture also allows for a relative equality of power between two parties. Individuals of different social locations or of unequal status even within the same culture can inadvertently work against one another. This is one of the difficulties of charitable work—to encourage people of means to help those in need without demeaning or disempowering the recipients of charity in the process. When some remain dependent on the largesse of others, the development of true partnership between them becomes elusive—even though both sides may desire it and strive for it.[5]

This is not to say that one should minister only with people of one's own culture or class or racial background. Quite the contrary! Indeed, such an insular approach to ministry has been a bane of congregational life in the United States throughout its history. Rather, it is important to notice that ministry across cultural contexts and divisions requires greater effort and cultural sensitivity than many expect when entering a ministry outside of their cultural comfort zones. It is laudable to step toward one's neighbors beyond cultural, economic, and racial barriers. The pages that follow should prove a helpful resource to this end, and more will be said about social location later. For now, it is important to notice that the social location of both agents and patients unavoidably shapes the moral meaning of individual actions.

In addition, besides the intended moral patient, there may be others who are affected by a given decision or action. Any but the most trivial actions might produce a ripple effect of consequences, and there may be many who become affected by that action. Who are they who bear the consequences of an action? Sometimes the most vulnerable can bear the weight of others' decisions. There is a proverb that is so generally true that it has become cliché: "When the elephants fight, it is the grass that gets trampled." Social location again becomes important. Are those who are actually affected by a decision recognized by the decision makers? If so, how is any risk of harm to them determined and then weighed? Are their values taken

---

5. Liedke, "Solidarity in Conflict," 78; Ramsbotham et al., *Contemporary Conflict Resolution*.

into account? Are they consulted so as to be empowered to participate in the decision?

Case for Reflection and Discussion

The Turkeys

Poverty was prevalent in the multicultural city of Costello, New Jersey, where Pastor Bryce served a small Methodist congregation. The population surrounding the church was approximately 30 percent African American, 30 percent European American, 30 percent Latino/Latina, and 10 percent Asian. Many depended on public assistance during a time in which both the federal and state governments were tightening their budgets. Pastor Bryce was a European American male from an upper-middle-class, suburban background. He had experience in urban ministry, though, and a sense of personal comfort in solidarity with the people of his parish.

Many members of this congregation were European American women heads-of-household and their children, who were living in situations characterized by poverty. The congregation sought to minister helpfully within this neighborhood and the entire city. They maintained a food pantry and a thrift store in order to provide food and clothing to neighbors in need. Even many members in the congregation itself required supplemental food each month. The ministry's motto, emblazoned on the letterhead, was a quotation from John 21:17: "Feed My Sheep."

The congregation found resources to support this ministry through a network of partnerships with suburban congregations. Some of these suburban communities were very wealthy—the homes for some corporate executives and even a former president of the United States. The suburban partners helped by providing financial resources and donations of food and clothing, and they also volunteered to work side by side in fellowship with the urban congregants.

While the need was continual, it was particularly noticeable during the holidays. Around the time of Thanksgiving and Christmas, the spirit of giving would particularly inspire people in the suburbs to share with people in the Costello parish. Sometimes, Bryce wished that this generosity would extend more evenly throughout the year, but he was grateful for donations whenever they were given.

Action and Reflection

One Thanksgiving, a suburban congregation offered to give the Costello parish twenty-five turkeys. The donor of the turkeys, though, wished to be able to deliver them personally to the needy families himself. He volunteered to accompany the pastor or one of the members of Costello parish in making these deliveries.

Pastor Bryce was unsure how to respond. He was very much aware of families who needed food and could use a turkey at Thanksgiving; some were members of his congregation but most were not. At the same time, he was feeling uncomfortable with the stipulation of the donor regarding personal involvement in the delivery. It felt somewhat intrusive on people's privacy. How might he proceed helpfully and respectfully? How should he respond to this offer?

Questions for Reflection

Analyze this case with respect to the individuals and institutions involved and their social contexts. Let the following questions serve as a guide.

First, what is the institutional context of the decision? What institution or institutions provide the framework for the pastor's decision? How are these institutions involved in presenting this opportunity for ministry? How are they involved in a regular way in ministry? How are they alleviating or aggravating the problem in question? How do they empower or delimit action or agency? How do they relate to each other? Do you know anything about their decision-making process or procedures?

Second, notice the people who are involved in this decision. The primary decision maker is presented as the pastor of Costello parish. Are there any other decision makers? How is the power to act occasioned by circumstance? By invitation? By institutional expectations? By privilege? How is the power to act limited? What are Pastor Bryce's choices? In what ways is he accountable for his choice, and to whom?

Who would seem to be the putative recipients of these turkeys? Can you describe aspects of their social location from the sketch provided above? Thinking about their social location, in what ways are you inclined or disinclined to accept the offer of turkeys and the manner of delivery?

Are there possible consequences to people beyond the twenty-five families who would receive a turkey? Who else might be affected in one way or another by this decision? Do you know anything about their social location or not? Would this be important for Pastor Bryce to take into account, or would the primary concern remain the twenty-five possible receivers of turkeys?

Having attended to the individuals and institutions involved in this decision scenario and their social contexts, now spend some time in explicitly theological reflection. Perhaps begin with the ministry's motto, "Feed my sheep." This quotation comes from the twenty-first chapter of the Gospel of John. What do you know about this passage? Who is presented as speaking these words in the Gospel? On what occasion are these words being spoken? To whom are these words being addressed within the biblical story itself?

Shifting attention from the story in the Gospel to the situation of ministry in Costello, who is assumed in the modern case to be the feeder of sheep? Who are assumed to be the sheep? Do you imagine Jesus still to be speaking in Costello? If so, from where, to whom, through whose voice, and about what? Has there been a tacit assumption that the poor of Costello are the sheep and that the privileged leaders of both congregations are the feeders of sheep?

Attend intentionally now to the poor parishioners themselves as those standing in line with Peter and as those now being addressed by Jesus's words from John's Gospel, "Feed my sheep." If these words are being addressed to the poor parishioners themselves (and not just or even primarily to Bryce and the donor), how do you start to interpret this passage newly? How do you find yourself thinking theologically about this context of ministry and this particular occasion for ministry?

Having thought through these different dimensions of this case, what ought Bryce to do? How do you find yourself reasoning in justification of this specific course of action?

Moral Dilemma

In analyzing this case, you would have undoubtedly entertained two options: (1) to appreciatively accept the offer of turkeys and make arrangements for the donor to assist in their delivery, or (2) to gratefully decline the offer—protecting the pride and privacy of people but foregoing this particular turkey meal for them. Each of these options, obviously, has trade-offs. This is why this decision-making scenario constitutes a moral dilemma.

A moral dilemma is a decision-making scenario in which there is a genuine moral argument in each direction. There is a real trade-off, in other words. The dilemma may constitute a mutually exclusive choice between two moral goods, neither of which can be fully realized along with the other. It may constitute a mutually exclusive choice between two evils, neither of which can be fully avoided along with the other. It may constitute a choice between two duties, neither of which can be fully followed along with the other. Thus a true moral dilemma differs from situations of moral confusion, in which the moral agent simply does not know what moral values or duties might be at stake. It also differs from situations of moral cowardice, in which the agent knows an action to be morally right but is afraid to move in that direction.

It is always desirable, of course, to look for other options. Are there third or fourth possibilities beyond the two initially envisioned? Perhaps one of these other possibilities is able to resolve the dilemma. At least, one of these possibilities might reduce the moral conflict to an acceptable level. One's moral duty can be argued to be that single course of action which is most consistent with one's values and which has the least dire trade-offs. At the same time, though, we have been suggesting that the values and perceptions of the moral patient are at least as important as the values and perceptions of the moral agent, and these may differ because of the differing social locations between the persons involved.

Sometimes, nevertheless, it is necessary to accept some of the trade-offs that present themselves in these kind of real-life situations. Third and fourth options should not be unrealistic imaginings of what might work in a more perfect world. It is not simply an academic exercise of seeking intellectual consistency, but of seeking consistency in order to be faithful to actual people, to be of real help to them, or to alleviate real suffering. In other words, sometimes it might be necessary to hold one's nose because it stinks to do so, but to proceed with the patronizing manner of distributing turkeys in order to alleviate people's real hunger. Conversely one might want to bite the bullet and forgo the turkeys, prepared to redouble one's efforts to find suitably festive protein for one's parishioners even though one might not be successful in doing so.

Further Questions for Reflection: Our Own Social Location

If you are discussing this case in a group, notice the differences in your group. Some will have valued the alleviation of hunger more. Some will have valued personal privacy more. Some will have placed in the foreground a particular reading of John's Gospel. Others will have let the contemporary context reshape different readings of the gospel passage. Some will have embraced the challenge to make a decision as a pastoral leader. Others will have wanted to engage a consultative process within the parish before reaching a decision. Some will have exercised a lot of leadership in the discussion itself—perhaps trying to argue one side or the other or perhaps trying to construct a third or fourth option. You will have noticed differences in opinions and values between you.

Now share with each other about your own social locations. What is it about your own culture or your own economic experiences that might incline you toward a particular interpretation of this case? Have you experienced racism or sexism in a way that now informs your interpretation of this case? Have you immigrated between different countries or cultures? How does your experience of immigration affect your understanding of this case? Perhaps as an immigrant, you have two very different but equally coherent interpretations of this case—one from the perspective of your culture of origin and one from the perspective of your current cultural home.

Notice within the group those who have been silent during the discussion. Ask them now for their opinions and insights. They may have complex thoughts that have needed time to take shape, or they may have a cultural heritage that values listening before speaking. What do they now have to say to the rest of the group?

If there is much diversity within your group, you will probably notice that differing moral and theological opinions have been shaped by people's different social contexts. This is not to say that people from a similar social context will necessarily agree with one another. Far from it! People from a similar social context often know how best to argue with each other. But their argument will proceed with a similar set of premises or assumptions grounded in a similar set of experiences and surrounded by a similar tradition and worldview. They know how to talk to each other, in other words. People from different social contexts may simply miss the import of each other's words because there may be fewer common points of reference. How might communication be facilitated in these kinds of circumstances?

Conclusion

Individual action takes place within a community of formative social forces and informative moral discourse. This powerful community shapes the individual and influences his or her decisions. This chapter has highlighted the importance of the social context of any particular decision and the social location of all individuals involved in a decision. Differing patterns of interaction between people of different social contexts create possibilities for both ministry and frustration, for both relationship and confusion, for both moral good and ill, for both liberation and oppression. These are opportunities to be embraced for the sake of the greater of the possibilities involved.

Ironically, even though we always know much more about our own social location than that of our neighbor, we can be less inclined to speak of our own. Often, we find that we are disposed to venture conjecture about our neighbors' values and motives and options instead. Yet it is most clarifying to speak of our own experiences and location in society. To clarify one's own background and interest gives space to the other to speak and can bring insight to both as a result.

Moreover, any observer of an action or decision will also be interpreting it in a manner informed by his or her own social location. This is true for scholarly as well as informal observers and writers in ministry, theology, and ethics. The social context of the observer or writer will be influential in a manner very similar to that of the moral agent and the moral patient described above. The observer's thoughts will be formed within a particular community of discourse. Writers in ethics or theology, for instance, might clarify the community of moral discourse that informs their writing, e.g. Western philosophical ethics, Roman Catholic natural law, and the like. Equally important as the community of discourse, however, are the myriad social forces that have also shaped an observer's very identity as well as his or her perceptions—experiences with poverty and wealth, with sexism and racism, with power and privilege.

From individual action we now turn to other levels of community that are involved in the practice of ministry. Three kinds of communities in particular provide the foci for the following chapters. There is the profession of ministry itself as a community of practice—much like other professional communities such as teachers or health care professionals. There is the church as community—particularly the congregation as the primary way of organizing the ministry of all believers as well as the ministry of professional clergy. Finally there is the wider community of which the church is a part—the "world" or "society" with its myriad forms of organization. The chapters that follow address each of these arenas of practice in turn.

2

Entering a Congregation's Culture

"Toto, I have a feeling we're not in Kansas anymore."
—DOROTHY

As THE DISCUSSION ABOUT social location unfolded in the previous chapter, the complexity of social location became apparent. This correlates with our complexity as human beings and the ways in which our individual identities are shaped in community. Moreover, we live as members of multiple communities, each of which is complex in its own right. A congregation is that type of complex community with its own structure of governance, circles of cliques, denominational connections, areas of intersection with its surrounding neighborhood, and missional bridges with the wider world. Moreover, members of any local congregation often come from other denominational traditions, other cultures, other communities and other countries. Together they constitute the community that is a congregation.

Social diversity is increasingly the norm even in smaller congregations. Of course, there are those longtime members whose children and grandchildren are baptized in the same congregation where they themselves were baptized. But many of these long-term congregation members have moved away from the home church and now commute to Sunday worship from elsewhere. Even long-term residents of a neighborhood parish who have not moved away, though, might watch as the community changes around them and as the congregation is challenged to adjust to these changes.

Entering a Congregation's Culture

At the same time that congregations are adjusting to social changes in their constituency and in their surrounding community, however, there is also inertia slowing the pace of this adjustment. The established culture of a congregation protects its identity in both overt and subtle ways amid social change. This is one of the impediments faced by congregations to becoming more truly multicultural. Newcomers frequently feel themselves to be just that—newcomers or visitors or strangers or outsiders—even when the congregation thinks of itself as welcoming, and even when the congregation is genuinely attempting to welcome others.

The passing of the peace is one such moment in many congregations. Ostensibly a community-building moment in which participants greet one another with signs of peace and reconciliation, it can also serve to demark insiders from outsiders and reinforce boundaries of congregational identity. Congregants might greet one another in ways that can be awkward for those who are new to the congregation—whether exuberantly with each other to the relative exclusion of the new person or, in the other extreme, physically affectionate to even the new person, who might not want to be hugged. Both patterns of greeting serve to establish congregational identity—take it or leave it.

It is into congregations as complex communities that pastors are called to leadership and service. Nancy Ammerman describes congregations as "subcultures within a larger culture." "One of your first tasks in understanding the culture of your congregation," Ammerman continues, "is to take an inventory of the important pieces of the outside culture your members share."[1] As subcultures, congregations can be seen to be situated within the larger culture and to reflect it in different ways. At the same time, as subcultures, congregations can be seen to attempt to distinguish themselves from the surrounding culture.

This and the following chapters explore aspects of congregational leadership informed by this cultural understanding of congregations. After defining *culture*, this chapter will attend to some of the dynamics of gaining access or entering a congregation's culture. The following chapter will explore these dynamics of entry further—recognizing that pastors can occupy both central and marginal positions at once within a congregation's culture. Chapters 4 and 5 will then introduce methods of reframing; these methods draw from institutional theory that interpret organizations in

---

1. Ammerman et al., eds., *Studying Congregations*, 78, 80.

terms of cultural dynamics. In the final chapters of the book, we will look at culture as a segue to and source for theological reflection.

Defining Culture

Culture is conceptually broad, making it difficult to define with precision. There are many definitions of culture providing particular emphases. *Culture* can be understood as synonymous with society or with civilization. Alternately it might refer to the greatest artistic achievements of that society or civilization. Or it can refer to commonplace patterns of meaning found in that society or civilization. There may be an emphasis on functioning and networks of social interaction or on symbolism and patterns of meaning making. There are nuanced definitions of anthropologists and commonsense definitions of people. Theologians and ministers use all of these definitions.

Moreover, even though we are all formed by and participate in culture, it can be difficult to identify our own culture. Ironically, our very familiarity with our own culture can make it hard to name. Terry A. Veling puts it this way:

> Part of the problem is that we are swimming in culture; it is like an ocean surrounding us, as water surrounds a fish. Or it is like the air we breathe. Or it is like a lens we see through, without us consciously noticing that we are wearing spectacles. Or it is like something entirely normal or 'natural' to us, even though to a person of a different culture it may seem quite strange and foreign.[2]

With this encompassing view of "culture," Veling is following Terry Eagleton and Raymond Williams in distinguishing between earlier and later usages of the word. In earlier usages, *culture* tends to refer specifically to intellectual, spiritual, and artistic developments and activities within society. A later usage of the word *culture*, however, refers to the totality of a social group's activities and way of life.[3] In this sense, it refers to "the entire way of life, activities, beliefs, and customs of a people, group, or society."[4]

---

2. Veling, *Practical Theology*, 159.

3. Eagleton, *Idea of Culture*, 1–9, citing Williams, *Keywords* (1976), 76–82; see also Williams, *Keywords* (1983), 87–93.

4. Smith, *Cultural Theory*, 2, citing Williams, *Keywords* (1976), 80.

Entering a Congregation's Culture

Earlier perceptions of culture gave way to the more holistic definition as cultural anthropology came to the fore in the twentieth century utilizing methods of participant observation for studying different cultures. The purpose of ethnographic study is to describe culture by observing people in the whole of their cultural context and by attending to the details of their existence together—their activities, their relationships with each other, their understandings of themselves and their way of life. All aspects of life within a given society were seen as culture. This is a very comprehensive understanding. This is the perspective of culture being assumed in the following pages as congregations are described as subcultures, as cultural communities, or as participating in culture.

Congregations as Cultures

In their primer for novice anthropologists, Julia G. Crane and Michael V. Angrosino recommend studying a congregation as an exercise in participant observation. They caution college students about the "culture shock" they might experience in entering a congregation and participating in a service of worship. Their caution is worth quoting as a reminder of how alien—or even alienating—congregational practices might be to those unfamiliar with them. They write:

> The first problem involved in this project will be facing what we have earlier defined as "culture shock." . . . do not be discouraged if you have a feeling of hopeless unfamiliarity at the beginning, a feeling that convinces you that there is something "wrong" going on in the service. Even so apparently trivial a matter as being confused as to whether one kneels, stands, or sits to pray can cause a certain degree of culture shock. The important thing is not to deny such ethnocentric feelings, but to accept them as natural and even to verbalize them, if you wish, to a sympathetic member of the congregation. Then you can begin to learn more about the sect, so that you can understand what is going on. Eventually, rituals that initially struck you as incomprehensible, ridiculous, or merely different will become meaningful to you.[5]

This is probably apt advice for new pastors and pastoral interns as well as college students. Even when we are generally familiar with patterns of congregational life and worship, the particular practices of any given

---

5. Crane and Angrosino, *Field Projects in Anthropology*, 68–69.

congregation can appear strange to us. New pastors might do well to pause reflectively in an attempt to understand these enigmatic practices before rushing to alter them to align with the pastor's preconceptions.

In fact the apparent strangeness when encountering a new culture is an opportunity for understanding it better. Some writers distinguish between "emic" interpretations of a culture, which seek to describe the culture as close to the perceptions of cultural insiders as possible, and "etic" interpretations, which seek to make sense of the culture using scholarly categories and theories that might apply across cultures.[6] Both an emic and an etic interpretation, though, can take advantage of the freshness of perspective that one brings to the culture as a participant observer. The observer as a newcomer is in a place to be able to attend appreciatively to the perceptions of cultural insiders. At the same time, the observer as an outsider is in a position to be able to organize his or her observations using categories of analysis that allow for deepening understanding and comparison across cultures. The opportunity for pastors to take both an insider's perspective and an outsider's perspective will be explored further in the next chapter with regard to the liminal status of clergy within the congregations they serve.

Jeffrey J. Ward and Oswald Werner cite Clyde Kluckhohn's analogy of "stereo vision" in voicing appreciation for the advantage of taking two perspectives into account when observing cultural phenomena. The analogy is one of depth perception. They write: "Just as the placement of our eyes gives us two perspectives which are combined to produce a perception of depth, so the ethnographer's stereo vision allows him [or her] to see more deeply into a culture than any single perspective could."[7] While this stereo vision pertains directly to the combination of insider and outsider perspectives that we have been describing, Ward and Werner expand the concept a step further. They suggest that this opportunity for depth perception is opened to us whenever we encounter enigmatic, anomalous, or discrepant phenomena that challenge our interpretation of a culture. When making observations of cultural practices and when interviewing cultural insiders about their understanding of cultural practices, it should not be assumed that all accounts will necessarily agree or that all of one's own observations will fit into a tidy pattern. Ward and Werner emphasize the importance

---

6. Luzbetak, *Church and Cultures*, 150, 225.

7. Ward and Werner, "Difference and Dissonance in Ethnographic Data," 104, citing Kluckhohn, *Mirror for Man*; see also Werner and Schoepfle, *Systematic Fieldwork*, 63.

of attending to anomaly as an "epistemological window" that can promote insight about a culture and deepen our interpretation of it. Anomalous accounts and events will challenge too reductionist an interpretation of the culture being observed.

Exercise for Reflection

Here is a summary of Crane and Angrosino's exercise for observing a congregation as a culture. This exercise is intended to promote skill in observation that would lead to inductive learning. Crane and Angrosino suggest making the following types of observations during a service of worship:

- The physical layout of the service: Where is it held? How is the room arranged? What furniture or other paraphernalia are present?
- The human dimension: how many people are attending? Relative numbers of men and women, adults and children? Physical characteristics of the participants? Interactions among participants?
- Aspects of ceremonialism: time of day? Specialized personnel? Special objects?
- The ceremony itself: who does what? When? What objects are used? How do people express their participation?[8]

A purely inductive approach to this kind of qualitative study would have the researcher make copious notes on his or her myriad observations of the congregation's practices. Then, in a subsequent step in the process of study, the researcher would review those field notes in order to inductively perceive patterns and themes apparent in them. These patterns and themes then become focal areas for yet another round of analysis of the field notes. An admittedly less objective shortcut, though, is to assume certain focal areas (such as focusing on patterns of welcoming and hospitality) from the outset.

Crane and Angrosino also suggest to their students that they identify "key informants" in the congregation whom they can interview asking, for instance:

- how they became members
- why they became members

8. Crane and Angrosino, *Field Projects in Anthropology*, 71.

- how often they participate

- whether they participate with family, with friends, or alone[9]

"You might also get these key informants to tell you what the ceremonies are all about," Crane and Angrosino continue, "You need not be concerned yet with whether their descriptions agree with yours, or whether the descriptions of ordinary members agree with those of the leaders."[10]

It is interesting that Crane and Angrosino caution their students that the "ordinary members" and the leaders of the congregation might differ from one another in their respective interpretations of the congregation's practices and ceremonies. As we might now expect, the differing social location of leaders and ordinary members within a congregation might dispose them toward such different interpretation even of their shared community. The next chapter and the remainder of this chapter will explore this relationship between pastor and parishioners further within a cultural frame of reference.

Pastoral Authority in Context

It can be a confusing, even a daunting, experience for pastors and pastoral interns to first enter a congregation's life and culture. The pastoral role within any congregation will be characterized by complexity and ambiguity. Part of this complexity is that pastors are expected to serve in many capacities: leading public worship, chairing meetings, offering pastoral care, engaging in community outreach, and the like. Individual pastors will have different degrees of confidence in these various activities. At a more general level, there is also ambiguity and complexity with regard to the pastor's authority and status in both the congregation and the surrounding community.

At one level, this confusion might indicate areas in which the new pastor or pastoral intern needs to develop skills, acquire knowledge, or deepen understanding. This is one level of reflecting on experience—learning the questions one needs to ask and then searching for the answers, or at least provisional answers, to those questions. Pastoral interns are usually equipped with a process for setting learning goals and assessing their learning.[11] Experienced pastors, too, benefit from bringing a similar

9. Ibid.
10. Ibid.
11. See especially Hillman, *Ministry Greenhouse*.

intentionality to their own contextualized learning in order to further their growth as adaptive leaders.

At another level, though, the confusion we experience in ministry may be indicative of the very real ambiguities, paradoxes, and ironies in the situation itself and in the role of being a pastor. The following pages examine some of the ambiguity concerning pastoral authority—addressing both those entering ministry for the first time and those who are well experienced in ministry. This ambiguity of pastoral authority is interpreted with reference to the pastor's paradoxical relationship to the congregation as both a cultural insider and cultural outsider at once. The question of pastoral authority provides a point of access to introduce the basic approach of reflective practice. The goal here is to deepen our self-understanding as we engage in ministry and as we encounter confusing or conflicting situations.

Many seminary interns in congregational ministry initially feel uncertain about their authority in their field placements. They compare themselves to their pastors and mentors, who are more established in their roles in these congregations. Curiously, though, many established pastors also experience uncertainty about their pastoral authority. Ironically, pastors are frequently cultural outsiders to their own congregations (at least to a degree) even while they play a central role in the congregation's leadership. This might be partly due to differences in social location between the pastor and parishioners. But, as we have seen, social location is not always identified simply. Our social location varies with each of the communities of which we are a part. In physical space, an object cannot be in two places at once. But in social "space," we seem to occupy multiple positions simultaneously. Marginality and centrality can both characterize a pastor's relationship to the congregation.

Writing with primary reference to the experience of Asian Americans and from his own personal experience, theologian Jung Young Lee affirms that one can be both marginal and central at once. One's relative marginality or centrality is in relationship to the various communities of which one is a part. One can be marginalized because of race or class or language in one context, but one can also be of high status or of central influence in another. Lee wants to help his readers not simply to be "in-between" different cultural worlds but rather to be "in-both." He hopes his readers can claim to be "in-both" cultural worlds with the advantage of perspective from both the margins and the center. Moreover, by the grace of God, he sees such richness of cultural experience to provide the opportunity to be "in-beyond" the narrow confines of any single cultural community. He speaks lucidly about the ambiguity of existing in more than one cultural community, about the ambivalence one might experience from being both respected and marginalized by others, and about possibility for creative and transformative response to marginality as well as centrality.[12]

As cultural insiders and cultural outsiders within their own congregations, pastors encounter both opportunities and limits to their pastoral authority. This quickly becomes apparent when a pastor is first called or appointed to a parish. That pastor faces the challenge of simply gaining entry and of being introduced to the congregation and the surrounding community. In being introduced to the congregation and community, the pastor paradoxically experiences both welcome and authorization, on the one hand, and the marginality of being a stranger or newcomer, on the other. Even after pastors have become well-established in their positions of ministry, dynamics of being cultural in-betweens continue to operate. These dynamics serve both to authorize our ministry as well as to limit that authority.

Welcome and Hospitality

As a point of comparison, let us consider other patterns of introduction. Communities establish cultural rituals for welcoming a newcomer into their midst. In some cultures, these rituals of welcome can be very elaborate and very rich. The welcome ceremony in Fijian culture is one such ritual, and it can provide a metaphor for understanding congregational welcome generally. Two aspects of a Fijian welcome particularly highlight the dynamics of entry into a community—the role of the hosts in welcoming a newcomer into their midst and the challenge faced by the newcomer to a culture to understand the cultural nuance of being welcomed.

The indigenous people of Fiji often refer to themselves as "people of the land." Upon entering a Fijian village or community, visitors are expected to present themselves to the village to be welcomed. Traditionally, they do this ritualistically by presenting a gift of *yaqona* to the people of the land. *Yaqona* is the root of a plant that is made into a beverage. The presentation of the gift, the preparation of the beverage and the imbibing by hosts and guests together are all accomplished ceremonially. Key to the ceremony of welcome is the role of the *matanivanua*—literally, "the face of

12. Lee, *Marginality*.

the land." This person serves as a mediator of communication—learning about the visitors in order to introduce them and their gift to the people of the land and, reciprocally, conveying the welcome and greeting of the land to the guests. The *matanivanua* seeks to ensure that the ceremony proceeds well, that the important information is conveyed, and that hospitality is extended. In other words, the *matanivanua* smooths the way for establishing relationship between the newcomers and the welcoming community.[13]

Not just in Fiji, I want to suggest, but in any culture or community and in any congregation, there are those who serve a role similar to that of the *matanivanua*. It can help the new pastor in entering a new place of ministry to look for these individuals and to allow them to facilitate one's welcome and one's initiation into the community. Sometimes this is formalized in congregations. Official greeters at worship services do this for visitors and all attendees. Many congregations also have a designated individual or welcoming committee to ensure visitors are warmly received. A new pastor will likely be introduced to the congregation by the chairperson of the staff-parish committee or the lay leader or another person in formal leadership in the congregation.

Individuals can also assume this role more informally. Some people are very well-connected in the congregation but may not be serving in a formal leadership role. Everyone, at least potentially, can introduce you to their friends and family and cohorts. One might do well to respect everyone in this capacity, but some individuals are particularly well-connected and can bridge between different communities. In fact, those most involved in the neighborhood and the life of the community beyond the congregation's walls may shy away from formal leadership in the congregation because they are already very busy within the larger social network.

Not just in the congregation but in the wider community—especially in the wider community—who are the *matanivanua*? Within the congregation, who helps to introduce the congregation as a whole to the wider community, and who helps to bring the wider community's concern to the attention of congregation? Also, perhaps entirely outside of the congregation, what individuals and what institutions present the "face" of this community? Again, this role can be formally established or more informally enacted. There are usually public-facing institutions in any community, though, with individuals ready to interpret their role and purpose in the community. The church is one of these, but so might be the chamber of

---

13. Tuwere, *Vanua*, 50, 72, 83.

commerce, the public library, the neighborhood association, the municipal or county administrative building, sporting clubs, singing organizations and jam sessions . . . The list continues. Informally, too, there are simply individuals who care about their neighborhood and show interest in their neighbors. They can help us ground ourselves in the culture of the community surrounding the congregation.

Of course in both the congregation and in the wider community, there may well be individuals who are more nosy than helpful or who may have their own agendas. One might not want to become too closely aligned with the first friendly face in either the congregation or the community. But one does want to avail oneself of the opportunity to welcome and to be welcomed. At both the formal level and at the informal level, I would look for these public-facing institutions and these welcoming individuals.[14]

If a pastor is to lead a congregation into meaningful and faithful ministry in the larger community, that pastor does well to start to get to know that larger community from the very outset of the pastor's ministry—simultaneously with (or even before) getting to know the congregation itself. Having grounded oneself in the community surrounding the congregation, one is actually better able to lead effectively within the congregation. It is like the buttresses on the wall of a cathedral; the cathedral's walls stand to house the congregation because they are buttressed in the land surrounding.

There are centripetal as well as centrifugal forces at work in the way we focus our energy in ministry; our attention is focused both within and beyond the congregation. Because of the complexity of congregations, though—programmatically, administratively, emotionally—a pastor can easily become entirely focused internally on congregational dynamics and on one's own sense of belonging within the congregation. This is a centripetal force on our attention as ministers. But to lead a congregation effectively in ministry to the wider community, the minister needs to be rooted in that larger community and its culture. Then we are better equipped to lead the congregation in an outward direction with the church›s ministry.

Reflective Exercise

Attend again to the congregation that you were observing gathered in worship. If you took field notes previously, you can first simply return to those field notes. Examine these notes again, looking for practices and symbols

---

14. Dudley and Ammerman, *Congregations in Transition*, 29–58.

of welcome and hospitality. That is, analyze the worship service of a congregation (including the physical layout, the human dimension, and the ceremony), being alert particularly to patterns of welcome and hospitality.

One might be attentive especially to ambiguity in these symbols—or of mixed signs of welcome and hospitality. (An example of such mixed messages of welcome might be rituals of friendship in which people are heartily welcomed from the pulpit and then asked to sign red attendance pads self-identifying as "visitor.") In particular,

- Can you identify ceremonies or rites of welcome (perhaps analogous to the Fijian welcome ceremony)?
- Who is being welcomed? Who is doing the welcoming? Are there people who seem distinctly unwelcome?
- Are there any who serve a mediating role in introducing people to the congregation or in introducing the congregation to new arrivals? (perhaps analogous to the Fijian *matanivanua*)?
  ◊ Is this role exercised formally or informally?
  ◊ Is this role always vested in the same individuals?

After reviewing your field notes focusing on this area of welcome and hospitality, make note of any patterns you may be discerning in this area. Write down any questions you might have concerning this area. Then, return to the congregation with these patterns and questions in mind for further observation. This time, perhaps, observe more broadly.

- In addition to the service of worship, are there other ways in which people interact with implications for welcome and hospitality?
- In addition to observing gatherings of the whole congregation, are there different groups in the congregation with their own patterns of welcome and hospitality (perhaps with different individuals serving roles like *matanivanua*)?
- Looking more broadly at the surrounding neighborhood or larger community, what are the places or the persons of connection between the congregation and the larger culture?
  ◊ Are there individuals in the congregation who are serving as bridge builders or communication conduits between the congregation and the surrounding community?

- ◊ Are there public-facing institutions in the surrounding community that seek to integrate newcomers into the community and its culture?
- ◊ Are there those in the surrounding community attempting to reach out to the congregation to integrate the congregation more fully into the wider culture?

If you identify people in welcoming roles (like *matanivanua*)—whether in the congregation or the surrounding community—who seem to be mediating communication between congregation and community, you might interview them. In this round of interviews, though, be sure to ask about the wider community and not than just the congregation. For example, you might ask:

- How did they become part of this neighborhood or community?
- Why do they participate in this neighborhood or community?
- How do they participate in this neighborhood or community (that is, what kinds of activities) and how often?
- What groups do they identify with in this neighborhood or community, e.g. friends, family, coworkers, fellow hobbyists, teammates, or the like.

Conclusion

The particular subject of welcome and hospitality has provided a lens through which to view congregations and cultural communities. As one gets to know the congregation as well as the culture of the surrounding community, one can begin to understand more about the congregation as a subculture of that larger community. One might attend to whether the congregation sees itself as representative of that larger culture or as more of a cultural outsider. One might notice ways in which the congregation sees itself as influential on the surrounding culture or more marginal in relation to it. Conversely, one might notice ways in which the surrounding culture influences the congregation. Moreover, these patterns of mutual influence between the congregation and the larger culture can be seen to change over time, with the contemporary relationship varying from historical patterns. We now turn to look in greater depth at pastors as both cultural insiders and cultural outsiders in the culture of the congregations they serve.

3

Liminal Leadership

Hospitality, therefore, means primarily the creation of a free space where the stranger can enter and become a friend instead of an enemy . . . [It is] the liberation of fearful hearts so that words can find roots and bear ample fruit. It is not a method of making our God and our way into the criteria of happiness, but the opening of an opportunity to others to find their God and their way.[1]

—HENRI NOUWEN

Liminality in Cultural Context

We have been using a cultural lens to look at congregations. Through this lens, we are able to see congregations as multicultural communities, and we are able to view them as cultures within larger cultures. Two points have so far been suggested for pastoral leadership. First, for those entering a situation of ministry, it is good to ground oneself in the cultures of the wider community as well as in the congregational culture. Second, as a step in that direction of inculturation,[2] it helps to notice those who can serve as the

---

1. Nouwen, *Reaching Out*, quoted in Nouwen, *Dance of Life*, 79–80.
2. "Inculturation" refers specifically to the cultural contextualization of theology and religious practice. As a missiological category it is distinct from the related anthropological ideas of "enculturation" (which refers to the process by which culture and cultural identity are transmitted to individuals within a particular culture) and "acculturation" (which refers to borrowing and influence between cultures). See Luzbetak, *Church and*

matanivanua—that is, gatekeepers to the culture who can actually help you open the gate. A third point will be the focus of this chapter. It is a caveat that we will always be relative outsiders when we are living in another culture. This is so even a long time after initial introductions have been made and relationships established. This applies to pastors within the cultures of their congregations. It applies to seasoned pastors as well as to interns.

Moreover, our leadership in ministry is a function of both the degree to which we are integrated into the host culture of our parish and the degree to which we remain relative outsiders. As cultural outsiders, we notice things which cultural insiders take for granted. At the same time, as strangers, we tend to miss much of the cultural nuance—and indeed the deep significance—of occurrences and events around us.

Returning to Fiji, again, and to the analogy of drinking *yaqona*, it is common for people to gather around the punch bowl of *yaqona* on many occasions besides the welcome ceremony. On an important occasion, everyone in a given community might be gathered around the punch bowl—men and women, young and old, hosts and guests, people of high status, such as tribal chiefs, as well as commoners. The circular seating around the punch bowl seems to indicate a commonality of all in community. Nevertheless, hierarchy is always present and is marked for all to see. Typically the round punch bowl, or *tanoa*, might have a front that is decorated by a large cowry shell and a braid of coconut fiber that extends toward the people of highest status. This hierarchical arrangement is obvious to all cultural insiders, but it is hidden from newcomers to the community.

On one occasion while I was teaching in Fiji—an important occasion in which the son of the principal of the seminary was being married—our newest colleague, who had recently arrived from a sister seminary in another culture, came into the circle; he conveyed his warm congratulations, and then naively turned (for what seemed like an eternity) with his rear end facing the principal and other honored guests while he spoke to others gathered in the circle. There was an audible intake of breath among participants. Could he not see that his posture was insulting those who were receiving honor on this occasion? Of course not! How could he? This is what drives one crazy in cross-cultural ministry. My spouse has said that cross-cultural ministry is learning how to be comfortable always making faux pas. The stress associated with constantly having to adjust to unarticulated cultural norms can lead to "culture shock." As a perennial guest, it is hard not to be

Cultures, 64–72, 308, 321–22.

a cultural klutz. One can never have the knowledge and cultural fluency of one's hosts. We depend on their gracious goodwill to receive us.

Similarly in pastoral ministry even in one's own country, to reiterate, pastors find themselves as cultural outsiders. Each congregation has its own traditions and customs, its way of seeing things as well as doing things, its way of making decisions and its way of making assumptions—including procedures and assumptions about the pastor. The pastor is in a liminal position within this congregational community. The word "liminal" comes from the Latin root *limen,* which means "threshold." In some significant ways, the pastor is always at the threshold of the congregation's subculture—both insider and outsider at once. The pastor is simultaneously both a central person with authority within the congregational community and a cultural outsider on the margins of that congregational community.

Much of the discussion about liminality is inspired by anthropologists studying rites of passage. Most notably, the very phrase "rites of passage" has become prominent in our discourse largely due to the study by Arnold van Gennep in a book by that title. Van Gennep studied rites of passage in various cultures as individuals were initiated from one role or status into another. He notes that individuals' experiences of passage can often be seen to move through three phases: (1) separation from previous role expectations, (2) liminality or transition, and (3) incorporation into a new status. The individual is removed from one set of cultural expectations during the initial phase of separation in order to enter the liminal or marginal phase in which the individual is in between sets of expectations. This liminal period, then, eventually resolves in a new aggregation of the individual's role within the community.[3] One can see this pattern operating in ordained ministry—not just expressed in the rituals of ordination and consecration as rites of passage but also exemplified in the real paradoxes of parish leadership that we have been discussing.

Van Gennep's work on rites of passage later inspired Victor Turner, who expounded and expanded on the idea of liminality in order to interpret various cultural activities. Turner studied pilgrimages, rituals, celebrations, and other cultural performances. He found a similar process to apply within many different cultural situations. Old structures dissolve (at least temporarily) initially as the community enters a liminal period in which there is greater freedom and creativity. This allows (again, at least temporarily) for a deeper sense of authentic community, which Turner terms

3. van Gennep, *Rites of Passage,* 10–11, 21.

"communitas." There is freedom and creativity during this liminal period; it provides the opportunity for the suspension of structure and hierarchy. This is especially the case, he notes, with regard to the status of people within hierarchical structures. Many disparate cultures, he finds, ritualize times in which hierarchy is dissolved or reversed, when the mighty are humbled and the humble act with authority. The period of liminality, though, eventually concludes with the establishment of structure—either with the reestablishment of expected patterns or with the emergence of new structures for the life of the community. Between old and new structures, though, there is freedom, creativity and a depth of community.[4]

Liminality and the Missional Church

Writing about the need for missional church leaders, Alan J. Roxburgh cites Turner in describing the liminal condition of churches in Western cultures. He describes two broad historical patterns of social change impelling this liminality. One is the loss of the central place of religion and religious authority in Western cultures and the dispersal of once-sacral symbols throughout more secularized usages and cultural practices. The other is the very shift of Western cultures from modernity into postmodernity with waning confidence in all metanarratives and a loss of any consensus about the constitution of a cultural center and periphery. The church's liminal position in society opens up new possibilities at the same time that former roles are foreclosed. "Liminality is also a place of opportunity, creativity, and transformation," assures Roxburgh. "In liminality we can recognize inappropriate metaphors and rediscover foundational symbols and images for the church and its leadership."[5] He calls for the development of church leadership that can be more attentive to our liminal situation at the edge of culture and to the opportunities for creative ministry entailed in the notion of communitas. He writes:

> Liminality requires leaders with the theological, political, and social skills to elicit the new communitas. This involves not just technique but the art of memory and expectation in which the lived experience of the past is indwelt in order for it to become our experience once more. This requires leaders whose identity is formed by the tradition rather than the culture. It also requires

4. Turner, *Ritual Process*, 94–130, 166–203.
5. Roxburgh, *Missionary Congregation*, 45.

leaders who listen to the voices from the edge. This is where the apostle, the prophet, and the poet are found. These are the metaphors for congregational leadership today. The pastor's ears must be attuned not primarily to the popular, the latest trend, or the expert, but to those who recognize that marginality is the church's reality.[6]

In fact, I want to suggest that the liminal nature of church in society and the liminal nature of pastoral authority within the church make the liminality of church leadership unavoidable. The question, it seems to me, is whether as individuals we embrace or resist this liminality and its creative potential for ministry.

Roxburgh subsequently reiterated his prescription for church leadership in *The Sky is Falling* but emended it in a way that is both suggestive and potentially confusing. He distinguishes in this subsequent book between two "tribes" named "Emergents" and "Liminals." While both are dealing with the same liminal realities in church and society, according to Roxburgh, "Liminals" are portrayed as facing the challenges of social change with a nostalgia for the church's historic centrality, and "Emergents" are portrayed as eschewing resources from the past in facing the present and future unfettered. He then suggests that the needed "communitas" is a more open dialogue between these two tribes. Roxburgh nevertheless recognizes that this portrayal is something of a caricature and that all of us have characteristics of each.[7]

Other writers about the missional church, though, have seized on the ideas of liminality and communitas in ways that seem to blur the more ephemeral and transitional nature of communitas. Alan Hirsh, for instance, seems to argue against Roxburgh when he insists:

> While some missiologists use this idea to describe the experience of transition the church in the West is currently experiencing in moving from one state (Christendom) or mode of church to another (missional), the emphasis has generally been on the new state of the church at the end of the process and so liminality and *communitas* are viewed as temporary experiences. From my perspective, significant manifestations of Apostolic Genius teach us that liminality and *communitas* are more *the normative situation and condition* of the pilgrim people of God.[8]

6. Ibid, 57.
7. Roxburgh, *Sky is Falling*.
8. Hirsh, *Forgotten Ways*, 222, citing Roxburgh, *Missionary Congregation*, ch. 2.

Part 1: Reflection on Practice

A subsequent text coauthored by Hirsh and Darryn Altclass carries this a step further programmatically, with "suggested habits and practices" to "encounter true *communitas*," developing a vision to lead a group "into genuine expressions of *communitas*," and even a grid for crafting action plans for achieving "authentic *communitas*."[9] My sense is that Roxburgh's treatment of the ideas of liminality and communitas in his *Missionary Congregation* is more consistent than these other subsequent developments with Turner's theory and the original use of these terms.

I want to emphasize here (1) that the very nature of liminality necessarily characterizes all parish clergy to some degree, and (2) that communitas provides for more authentic relationship and greater creativity made possible by liminality and the fragmentation of traditional expectations. Communitas is not a programmable end-state that can be successfully structured into the church's ongoing life as an institution; it is rather the result of liminality and the abeyance of structure and role expectations. New structures might be created during the liminal period (or new iterations of old structures might return), but communitas is a function of the in-between state.

Liminality and Pastoral Authority

George B. Thompson Jr. examines the ambiguous nature of pastoral authority in a way that can be seen to be related to the pastor's liminal status as we are here understanding it. Thompson uses the language of "adoption" to describe the gradual acceptance by congregants of a pastor and of that pastor's authority. Thompson describes the process by which pastors are increasingly accepted, trusted, and empowered by a congregation as "creating cultural capital for doing ministry." Yet, when a contentious issue arises, Thompson reminds, even a well-loved, trusted, and "adopted" pastor can suddenly find himself or herself on the outside again, marginalized by lay members who have comparatively deeper roots in the congregation. Much success in pastoral leadership, according to Thompson, is in the pastor honoring this gatekeeping function of respected members of the congregation. Such a pastor is able to build trust patiently within the cultural community. A pastor sensitive to these dynamics knows that he or she can suddenly

---

9. Hirsh with Altclass, *Forgotten Ways Handbook*, 175, 177, 187.

be thrown into relative marginality again even after having been implicitly authorized or tacitly "adopted."[10]

While liminality characterizes the position of pastors within the cultures of their congregations, this relative marginality of a pastor's authority, I want to suggest, often goes unnoticed or at least unacknowledged. The pastor's marginality can be belied or hidden by other aspects of the pastoral relationship. Three in particular are (1) assumptions of cultural similarity between the pastor and the congregation, (2) the counterbalancing realities of pastoral authority over and against marginality, and (3) an ethos of unity within the congregation. Each of these will be discussed below.

First, a pastor's marginality within a congregational culture might be camouflaged by cultural similarities between the pastor and the congregation. Frequently the pastor is serving in a congregational subculture that resembles the pastor's own culture of origin rather than in a culture that is entirely strange to the pastor. When a pastor is serving in a more obviously cross-cultural situation, such as illustrated by the above example about drinking *yaqona* in Fiji, one is constantly reminded that one is an outsider. There is a lack of familiarity with cultural practices—perhaps even with the language itself. Even when one does become more familiar over an extended period of time with a different culture's practices, there can still be reminders from cultural insiders that one is a cultural traveler with roots in another way or another place. Long-term residents who have emigrated from one country to another in order to make their home in a new place can find these reminders to be irritating and insulting. "How long," one wonders, "must one live in this land and bear children within this land before one is fully accepted by one's neighbors in this land?" Still, immigrants learn to read these signals from their neighbors and to use them to help navigate successfully within the host culture that is now their home even when they are ambiguously welcomed.

When one moves between subcultures of an overarching culture, however, the differences can be more subtle and nuanced. The more similarity there is between subcultures, the more hidden might be the cultural differences that remain. Such similarities might be a common language, a common religious tradition, a common historical heritage, or a common denominational polity. Yet even with these similarities, there can be differences in local customs, traditions, ethos, and expectations that limit a pastor's acceptance within a community and constrain the pastor's authority in

---

10. Thompson, *How to Get Along with Your Church*.

that community. These cultural differences are more easily noticed if they are expected. One can more easily see them, in other words, if one looks for them.

Also, social location comes into play as a potential hindrance to the sensitivity needed for observing cultural difference. When a pastor is accustomed to occupying a culturally privileged position within a subculture, and when that subculture is itself the dominant culture within its society, it can be all the more difficult for that pastor to check his or her perceptions. A pastor's privileged position might not predispose that pastor to perceive cultural differences or to interpret such differences as deviations from the pastor's own cultural norms. From such a presumed position of privilege it is difficult to appreciate one's own marginality in other people's culture. In other words, we often just don't get it.

Second, quite simply, a pastor's marginality is held in balance with the pastor's authority in the congregation and the community. Whatever the formal denominational authorization of the pastoral office, every pastor does assume a central role and status within the congregation where she or he serves in ministry. Though people might interpret pastoral authority differently, this central position of the pastor is visible to members of the congregation as well as to those beyond its walls. Indeed, the pastor is often the representative face of the congregation to the surrounding community. People associate pastors with their congregations and vice versa, and authority is often more obvious than marginality to people viewing the pastor in relation to the congregation.

These representational and relational aspects of pastoral authority are emphasized by Jackson Carroll. According to Carroll, authority is relational in character. The "ultimate basis of authority" within any given group of people, writes Carroll, is that the leader "is granted authority to lead because she or he is believed to protect, interpret, and represent the group's core values and beliefs and contribute to their realization."[11] Authority, in other words, is authorized—whether formally or informally, tacitly or explicitly. It has to do with the actual relations between people and the ways they organize their life together. Interns, for instance, are often surprised at some point during their internship when they realize that congregants are regarding them not as students but as ministers; the informal and tacit authorization by congregants can occur ahead of (and anticipate) the formal authorization of ordination.

---

11. Carroll, *As One with Authority*, 43.

For pastors and congregations, relational authority has to do with mutual expectations about the ways they organize their life together to express their faith with each other and in the wider community. Tensions can arise when those expectations are not mutually held. One set of expectations might have to do with the areas in which the pastor is assumed to have expertise, skill, or professional competence.[12] Another set of expectations, though, has to do with the representational nature of pastoral ministry—representing both the community that "authorizes" and the sacred traditions of that community. Carroll emphasizes this *sacral* dimension of pastoral authority, even though he recognizes that many pastors are uncomfortable with it. He writes: "If we have authority as clergy, it is because laity perceive us to be reliable interpreters of the power and purposes of God in the context of contemporary society. And this involves both spirituality and expertise, not one without the other."[13] Pastoral authority represents both the authorizing religious community and, in bolder words, their God.

Some pastors are uncomfortable with this authorization, this popular regard and respect for their office. Others, conversely, can be uncomfortable with their relative lack of authority and their marginal position within a congregational culture. Moreover, many pastors are ambivalently uncomfortable with both their authority and their marginalization. They can feel ambivalent, in other words, with regard to this very ambiguity in their role and status. Paradoxically, both do apply; both authority and marginalization characterize the pastor's relationship with parishioners within a congregational culture. Moreover, the visibility of pastoral authority can obscure the reality of the pastor's marginality within a congregational culture.

Third, there is often an ethic of love, acceptance, and unity that pervades the way people want to regard their relationship with each other and with their pastor. This ethos of unity disinclines us to perceive difference. People and pastor alike do not necessarily want to notice their cultural difference or the fact that they may be significantly different from one another. We want to sing "We Are One in the Spirit" and celebrate our unity without necessarily noticing our differences. Yet difference must be perceived in order to be celebrated. Without noticing and respecting our cultural differences, we fill in the gaps of mutual understanding with inference, assumption and even prejudice. We then risk running into one another's unshared

---

12. I discuss the professional competence of pastors in relationship to congregations more thoroughly in Bush, *Gentle Shepherding*, 58, 115–16, 153–54.

13. Carroll, *As One with Authority*, 54.

assumptions, frustrating each other's expectations, and making deeper community elusive. This is so for all cultural differences within a congregation and is not limited to the relationship between pastor and parishioners.

In his study of multicultural congregations, Charles R. Foster has noticed that cultural differences between people in a congregation provide a temptation to people of the majority to attempt to assimilate people of minority cultures. The attempt is to erase difference by forming a more unified congregational culture. Indeed, one key strategy of the "church growth" movement of previous decades has been to take advantage of this tendency of people toward a homogeneous culture by encouraging the development of culturally homogeneous congregations. In contrast, though, Foster notices that the members of congregations seeking to be truly multicultural must constantly recognize and negotiate their respective differences.[14]

Similarly, in her study of twenty-three congregations facing social changes in their surrounding communities, Nancy Ammerman has noticed that congregations able to adapt constructively and to embrace social changes were marked by internal conflict during the periods of transition and change; none of the non-adaptive congregations she studied experienced such conflict.[15] One lesson that can be drawn from these studies is that the skill for embracing cultural differences requires the development of a concurrent ability to deal with the constant tensions that inevitably arise as people gather and their cultural patterns vary. This is no facile unity. It is a dynamic forming of community. In such authentic encounter between cultures, the entire congregational community enters a liminal or marginal state as new community takes shape.

Liminality occurs in transition or passage from one place to the next or from one status to the next or from one kind of relationship to another, or from one way of being to the next. It has to do with our very sense of personal identity as individuals living within a community as we transition within that community. It can also have to do with our corporate identity in situations of social change or congregational transitions. During a time of substantial or rapid change, we are noticing, a whole congregation or even a whole community might enter a liminal period—a time of dynamic movement between one state of affairs and the next, between one structure of leadership and another, between an earlier cultural constituency and a

---

14. Foster, *Embracing Diversity*, 13–16, 22–23, 36–47.
15. Ammerman, *Congregation & Community*, 334–35.

newer one, between one institutional role within the community and a different role, or even between a prior central role and recent invisibility.

Liminality can be transformative. It indicates dynamism in the community's relationships and the community's identity. For pastors, being both an insider and an outsider can empower leadership and shape ministry. The very tension between authority and marginality provides a creative opportunity for new forms of leadership and service. While one is in between, there is an element of indeterminacy, of freedom, of movement, of possibility, of openness, of change. The necessity of inherited expectations and structures become backgrounded during the liminal time, and the new expectations or structures are not yet created, articulated, or developed. Moments of liminality can be moments of creativity.

Case for Discussion

One summer evening after dark, Rev. Oliver was surprised to find Stanley ringing the front doorbell of the parsonage. Stanley was an older parishioner who lived on the other side of the city and who did not have a car. He must have walked the distance.

According to others in the parish, Stanley had always been a simple man but of limited intelligence. Most recently, he had been attending carefully neither to his personal hygiene nor to his financial situation. He had stopped paying rent at the YMCA where he had been boarding, even though he had limited but sufficient income to pay the rent. Finally, it seems, he had been evicted from his room and had nowhere else to turn. It was too late to get into the shelters in town. Besides, Stanley indicated that he had tried to stay at these shelters but that he had been turned down. This seemed odd to Rev. Oliver, but Stanley was not very articulate concerning these circumstances.

"I don't know," he replied to most of Rev. Oliver's questions.

Why were you evicted?

Why wouldn't the shelter take you?

Have you been in touch with your caseworker, and how has she advised you?

Is your caseworker going to help you to find shelter?

Where do you think you can stay tonight?

Part 1: Reflection on Practice

"I don't feel very good," Stanley told Rev. Oliver, but returned to his theme of "I don't know" when asked about his particular symptoms. "I just don't feel very good," he said.

If he is sick, Rev. Oliver thought, he needs health care, and he certainly doesn't need to stay on the streets. Perhaps he should go to the hospital, Rev. Oliver reasoned, where he could be diagnosed, find a place to rest, and get back into the system and to the attention of his caseworker. When asked if he would like to go to the emergency room of the local hospital, Stanley responded with a definite yes. So, they got into Rev. Oliver's car and went to the hospital.

Once in the emergency room of the hospital, however, Stanley was no more articulate concerning his particular symptoms. He reiterated to the health care professionals that he did not feel very good but would not identify the first symptom.

The emergency room was busy. Many of the financially poorer residents of this city used the emergency room as their primary provider of health care.

"I'm sorry," Stanley and Rev. Oliver were told, "there is nothing we can do if you can't tell us what is wrong." They were sent away.

Getting back into the car, Rev. Oliver decided to try a different hospital in a different community about a half-hour's drive away. He knew of a county hospital in an adjacent county that had excellent geriatric facilities. It was located in a much more affluent county, so there might not be the same financial constraints that had most likely been a factor in their reception at the city's local hospital. Also, it was located in a less populated area, so the emergency room would surely be less crowded.

Rev. Oliver's speculation proved to be accurate. After arriving at the emergency room for the hospital in the adjacent county, they found themselves the only ones seeking help that night. The health care professionals were courteous and respectful, even warm in their welcome. They agreed to examine Stanley, even though he was only minimally articulate about how he felt.

After examining Stanley, they discovered that he was infested with lice. (This might have something to do with his eviction from the YMCA and his lack of welcome at the shelters, Rev. Oliver realized.) The health care professionals then proceeded to give Rev. Oliver a solution with which to bathe Stanley once they returned home, in order to rid him of the lice.

"No, thank you," Rev. Oliver responded politely. Then turning to Stanley, Rev. Oliver explained: "They've figured out what's wrong, Stanley. I'm going to go now. They should take care of you here. If they don't, just find a comfortable spot here on the grounds for the night. I'll check up on you in the morning."

"Yup, thanks, Olly, thanks a lot," Stanley agreed readily. He seemed to Rev. Oliver to both understand his situation and to appreciate this provisional solution to his problem. "They'll take care of me," he agreed.

"What!" the staff exclaimed. "You can't do that! You can't leave him here. Call security!"

"Good night now, Stanley," Rev. Oliver said. "I'll see you tomorrow."

"Good night, Olly," said Stanley. "Thanks, again."

Rev. Oliver strolled out, knowing that security could not stop him, knowing that Stanley was in better hands at least for the moment, and knowing that he had upset some very nice people indeed.

The next morning, Rev. Oliver called Stanley's caseworker to inform her of Stanley's whereabouts. "I know exactly where Stanley is," she said with a chuckle. "They called me first thing this morning. How in the world did you get him over there?"

"I just took him," Rev. Oliver replied. "I hope I didn't get you in trouble."

"Oh no," she reassured him. "This is fine" she said. "We'll be able to take care of him now, but I could never have done that myself."

In the days ahead, Stanley's caseworker was able to place him in a residential home or halfway house that allowed him considerable autonomy but that assisted him with his self-care. Stanley continued to attend the congregation where Rev. Oliver was the pastor. He usually rode the church bus, but sometimes he still chose to walk all the way across the city.

Discuss this case giving attention to the ideas of structure and liminality.

What structures are in place providing parameters for this situation? That is, what institutions and institutional expectations seem to be determining possibilities as well as constraining choices for the people involved? For Stanley? For Rev. Oliver? For the health care professionals at the city hospital? For the health care professionals at the county hospital? For Stanley's caseworker? Who seems to have power within these institutions? How are these individuals empowered? Conversely, how is their power limited, defined, channeled, or constrained? Do there seem to be cultural assumptions operating in these definitions of power?

Who is marginal or liminal in this scenario? That is, whose possibilities for action seem to slip between the structured expectations of different institutions and roles? In what ways is Stanley a liminal figure? In what ways is Rev. Oliver liminal? Are the health care professionals liminal? Is the caseworker? Notice that liminality is not simply about the power to act or not to act within a situation but about a freedom to act in creative ways, which comes from being somewhat outside established expectations.

Liminality and Pastoral Care

In discussing the above case as it pertains to pastoral care, power and powerlessness can be seen to be operating in many ways—some expected and some not expected ways, perhaps even in contradictory or ironic ways. Rosita deAnn Mathews writes about the possibilities of "using power from the periphery." As a hospital chaplain, Rev. Mathews worked within a hospital setting that perpetuated a status system with medical expertise being central and with other forms of caregiving relatively marginalized. She writes of defining her own importance for spiritual care within this context:

> Rather than assigning a less important status to my function, I have exercised my pastoral authority in my work. I have attempted to provide a place for the divine-human encounter that can often happen when one is placed at the edge of health and, ultimately, of life. Within those moments, I journey with those who are asking questions about the deeper meanings of life and existence.
>
> Using this pastoral authority has put me at odds with physicians whose call is to preserve life at all costs.[16]

Moreover, as an African American woman, she had experience of marginalization within society as a whole and an understanding of the possibilities of a powerful yet vulnerable periphery. As she became director of pastoral services within a Veterans Administration hospital, she writes of choosing to continue to exercise her peripheral power within the system itself. She explains:

> How does one exercise power from the periphery? It is done by refusing to employ destructive tactics when one works from within

---

16. Mathews, "Using Power from the Periphery," 100.

a system. It is refusing to fight evil with evil. It is using one's position to further the greater good and speak truth on behalf of the individual. It is choosing to operate within an ethical framework and to nurture personal spirituality. It is choosing to do what is right or, at least, what is best. Using power from the periphery also means accepting the consequences of not doing politics according to the system's rules.[17]

"To do this successfully," Mathews continues, "we must realistically assess our need for power, promotion, and acceptance. We must redefine success and not let the system define it for us."[18]

There would seem to be two entwined elements articulated in Mathews's advice here. First she advocates realistic self-assessment with regard to one's own understanding of and need for power and status. Second, she would have us claim the opportunity to "redefine success" for ourselves even when operating within larger organizational systems that might entail their own conceptual frameworks, value systems, and expectations about authority. She combines, in other words, both (a) realistic self-awareness and (b) conceptual reframing of our understandings of power and authority, periphery and center.

Such attentiveness to both self-awareness and conceptual reframing, I would add, opens up possibilities for relating to others more genuinely across social divisions within an organizational context. It allows for both greater self-understanding and deeper understanding between people. It allows for both recognition of our commonality and appreciation of differences between us. Notions of power and periphery, of success and status, can be interpreted as metaphors for expanding the horizon of human relationships rather than restricting our interactions more literally to institutional roles and expectations.

Victor Turner has remarked on the liminal capacity of metaphors and models to turn our expectations about social events or about the social world. Regarding metaphorical thinking, Turner writes that the "combination of familiar and unfamiliar features or unfamiliar combination of familiar features provokes us into thought, provides us with new perspectives," and he adds, "the implications, suggestions, and supporting values entwined with their literal use enable us to see a new subject matter in a

---

17. Ibid, 101.
18. Ibid, 102.

new way."[19] Rosita deAnn Mathews provides such a creative "unfamiliar combination of features" when she describes power from the periphery. This unexpected combination of ideas opens possibilities for reconceiving both power and periphery, informing pastoral practice in new ways.

Writing about pastoral theology and pastoral care, Pamela Cooper-White invokes Turner's understandings of liminality and metaphor to urge the development of a "thick theory" of pastoral counseling. The liminal potential in metaphorical thinking, she opines, opens a multiplicity of perspectives on oneself and others and on God. "A view of both God and persons as multiple," she writes, "is intended to promote a theology and an anthropology that is enlarging, empathic, and life enhancing." To recognize and engage the multiplicity in others, according to this perspective, it is helpful to recognize the multiplicity and complexity in oneself. To know this complexity, to see this multiplicity in both self and others, broadens our framework for interpretation and action.[20]

In actual pastoral encounters, though, how do we access this expanded interpretive horizon in order to inform our pastoral practice? In most situations of pastoral encounter, we respond to each other quickly and intuitively—framing the situation in accordance with whatever assumptions we happen to bring. We respond to one another's words as we hear them—as we understand their literal meaning and as we understand them within our own symbolic frame of reference. It takes effort, though, to begin to hear more authentically from the other's perspective, to adopt (at least provisionally) the other's symbolic frame of reference, to accept (at least provisionally) the other's assumptions. It takes effort because these levels of meaning and interpretation lie hidden from our direct observation. It takes time as well as effort to build the kinds of relationships that establish a more mutual understanding and to affirm a shared world of meaning. Moreover, it takes imagination as well as effort even to move in this direction, to begin to discern and discover another's worldview. It requires that we imagine the possibility that the speaker might be intending many meanings beyond our immediate ken.

We always interpret language, symbols, and events from within the cultural communities that give meaning to these symbols and events. This is what both isolates and connects us in our intersubjectivity. We can never be sure that we share entirely the same culturally constructed conceptual

---

19. Turner, *Dramas, Fields, and Metaphors*, 31.
20. Cooper-White, *Braided Selves*, 10, citing Turner, *Dramas, Fields, and Metaphors*.

framework, but at the same time we also can be confident that we do in fact share some of the same culturally shaped conceptual space. When two people meet, we can often forget that they bring their entire cultural communities with them in their respective understandings. We see two distinct individuals. It takes an imaginative leap to remember that their respective cultural communities accompany them in their understandings and in their responses to each other. With this perspective, though, we see that we are always "cultural outsiders" to another's world of meaning—even while we find ourselves "inside" the same immediate cultural context with each other. We listen more carefully, I would suggest, when we recognize our own liminal place as listeners and when we respect the other's relatively privileged position as speaker attempting to convey her or his understanding to us.

This communal nature of interpretation is emphasized in H. Richard Niebuhr's definition of moral responsibility. Niebuhr defines responsibility as follows: "The idea or pattern of responsibility, then, may summarily and abstractly be defined as the idea of an agent's action as response to an action upon him in accordance with his interpretation of the latter action and with his expectation of response to his response; and all of this is in a continuing community of agents."[21] There are four aspects of this definition of responsibility. There is, first, the recognition that a person's action is in response to an event or action. There is, second, the acknowledgment that this responsiveness is not simply mechanical but a matter of a person's interpretation of the preceding action or event. Third, we anticipate that our own responsive actions will be met by responses from others. Finally, fourth, there is the affirmation that all such interactions and interpretations are occurring within community and culture.

It follows, then, that all actions and responses—all interpretations and meanings—can be seen to be in dynamic flux according to the cultures being encountered and according to the encounters between cultures. When any two individuals form a relationship, they carry with them their respective cultural communities and the corollary cultural understandings of those communities. This multiplicity of meaning is especially apparent with religious discourse. Religious language is rich. A religious metaphor is symbolically polyvalent. It cannot mean just one thing. The trouble is, we tend to eisegete religious language, reading our own meaning into others' statements. This can be problematic for effective communication, making it

---

21. Niebuhr, *Responsible Self,* 65.

difficult both to understand the other's meaning and to respond with openness to the other. This is also one of the reasons why Christians of different denominations—like Christians of different cultures—can find themselves in confusing disagreement with each other even when they may be using the same language of faith and speaking the very same words.

This point was brought home to me by a number of hospital chaplains and CPE (Clinical Pastoral Education) supervisors working in one of the hospital systems in the Midwest. These chaplains and supervisors tended to be on the more liberal end of the theological spectrum, but they found themselves needing to communicate with more fundamentalist and evangelical students whom they were supervising. These students were from different denominational traditions, and some were from countries and cultures other than the United States. They utilized religious discourse to describe and to process the new experiences they were having in hospital chaplaincy. Such language of faith is not always defensive and indicative of resistance to learning—though it can often be so. Use of familiar religious language also allows students to assimilate new information into their religious worldview. Moreover, such use of language can even help students begin to accommodate their worldviews to new experiences and ideas. The chaplains and CPE supervisors were being challenged, however, to discern when such religious language was expressing a student's learning and growth and when it might be indicative of resistance and defensiveness. At the time, I was seeking to assist them in this endeavor. The following Practical Hermeneutics Grid was developed in that context.

In his book, *Practical Hermeneutics*, published in 1980, Charles E. Winquist attempts to recover and reclaim religious discourse and theological interpretation for pastoral care and pastoral theology. He wants to move beyond that which is directly observable and verifiable, and he says this about religious language:

> The discovery of the symbol is a crack in the surface of experience. This crack is threatening when we are satisfied with the depth that we have achieved in our understanding. The symbol can be simply defined as an expression that has more than one meaning. The discovery of the symbol is the recognition that some expressions are inherently ambiguous because they are valenced for more than one pattern of meaning. We can say that they are ambivalent or even multivalent.[22]

---

22. Winquist, *Practical Hermeneutics*, 31.

> The symbol reveals that every individual is living a multiplicity of stories that consciously intersect in the function of the symbol. Without the overinterpretation of symbolic language the presence of the symbol frustrates understanding. Overinterpretation is the implementation of a practical hermeneutic.[23]

Inspired by Winquist's practical hermeneutics, the following interpretive grid is meant to assist with such "overinterpretation" in search of better understanding. Each box on this grid invites us to brainstorm in an attempt to expand our understanding. What are the different possibilities involved for interpreting any phrase of theological conversation between two individuals. This might be especially helpful for interpreting those hot-button key phrases that tend to set us off because we already carry a charged interpretation of them. How might we begin to reexamine such theological phrases in light of their multiple meanings, taking into account differences between cultural communities?[24]

---

23. Ibid., 32.
24. Bush and Withers, "Which Religion Is Better?" 133–34, 137.

Part 1: Reflection on Practice

Practical Hermeneutics Grid For Facilitating Cross-Cultural Communication

Phrase in Question	
Possible meanings **the speaker** might bring	Possible meanings I **the listener** might bring (both intellectually and viscerally)
Possible **similarities** between us	Possible **differences** between us
My possible **responses** to this phrase	Which of my possible responses would be **most generous** to the speaker?
Contextual/cultural factors shaping the meanings in the encounter	

Exercise for Reflection

Remembering a point of theological confusion, religious misunderstanding, or perhaps even conflict between yourself and another, use the practical hermeneutics grid to analyze possible meanings and responses. To use the grid, identify and write the key phrase or symbol to be interpreted in the box at the top. Then fill in the remaining boxes with as many possibilities as you can imagine. The box at the bottom is simply to record contextual factors you notice that might be relevant to your mutual understanding or misunderstanding. The rest of the boxes pose questions directly to your respective understandings and to the possibilities of response: What are the possible meanings the speaker might bring to this phrase? What are the various meanings that I, the listener, bring to this phrase? How do I understand particular words in this phrase intellectually or respond to them emotionally? What are the apparent or potential similarities and differences between me listening and the person speaking? What are the various possibilities of my responding to the other. Then, given these possible responses, the grid asks me to choose that which seems to me to be the most generous option. This gives the other the benefit of the doubt in our encounter and gives me the chance to respond to that person with grace.

Conclusion

Both the pastor's authority and the pastor's marginality are opportunities for insight and creative ministry. In fact, they can be seen in mutual relationship with each other. As we have noticed, a pastor's actual authority is necessarily shaped by a relatively marginal position in the congregational culture, and this marginal position can in turn be reinforced by the pastor's peculiar kind of authority. The pastor's cultural position as a relative outsider we have described as liminal. This liminality, this in-betweenness, is both an occasion for confusion and for insight. It is also importantly an opportunity for creativity. To be on the threshold, as we have been discussing, is to be on the border between outside and inside. This gives one a unique perspective on both the inside and the outside of a culture or a congregation at once.

We have also noticed that pastors can have conflicting attitudes toward their own authority. Informed by a deepening appreciation for liminality, we are helped to interpret the clergy's ambivalence about pastoral authority.

Part 1: Reflection on Practice

We begin by clarifying the apparent contradiction. We have noticed that many pastors and seminarians are intellectually uncomfortable with the clergy's authority for good theological reasons, such as a commitment to community, a theology of empowerment, and an ethos of love. In apparent paradox, however, these same clergy and interns simultaneously can be discomfited at a personal level when our leadership seems ineffective, when we feel our ideas are not welcomed, our contributions accepted, or our personal integrity respected. At such times, when self-awareness about one's own functioning within the community is most needed, such self-awareness can be truncated by the disconnection between our best beliefs and values and our experienced practice. There is disjunction between our experienced need for respect of our pastoral authority and our espoused theology of ministry that minimizes pastoral authority.

The methods of reflective practice that I am introducing in this and the next chapter provide tools for clergy and for interns to attend realistically to our own functioning in confusing situations. Such clarity about our own functioning in ministry includes both our marginality in the congregational culture and our authority in that same culture.

4

Reflective Practitioners

WHAT MARVELOUS CONTRADICTIONS WE have been entertaining! Pastors are both central and marginal with regard to their authority in congregations. They are at once representatives of their congregations and cultural outsiders within those same congregations. Congregations desire unity in the Spirit but find that assimilative tendencies toward uniformity only frustrate the formation of deeper fellowship. A fuller fellowship between peoples of different cultures ironically entails constant tension and requires the skill of constructively negotiating inevitable conflict amid this tension. To move into such fuller fellowship amid difference requires able leadership, but we are noticing that the most obvious leaders, the pastors, are the very ones whose authority can be limited by a frequently unacknowledged marginality within the very congregations where they are called to serve as leaders. How are we to understand these ironies and apparent contradictions?

These ironies and apparent contradictions point to the need for a method to encourage deepening self-awareness for pastors while they are engaged in the practice of congregational leadership. Fortunately, they also provide the beginning of such a method. Noticing the contradictions in one's social context can provide the beginning of a deepening critical consciousness. Moreover, these contradictions can provoke a more creative response to those contradictions and can present the opportunity for new forms of community to arise.

The work of Paulo Freire provides an example of the educational and practical value of noticing contradiction. His book *Pedagogy of the*

Part 1: Reflection on Practice

Oppressed, published in English in 1970, has proven influential for both educators and theologians over the years. The word "conscientization" has entered the English vocabulary largely through his efforts. Freire's work that informed this book was to teach adult literacy in Latin America—a task in which he achieved remarkable success. A key dimension of his method was to help learners notice the contradictions in their own worlds and to name these contradictions. This critical consciousness, "conscientization," provided the motivational impetus for learners simultaneously to develop further facility with the language and to claim their own agency to name and to act on the social realities with which they were being challenged.

Noticing and naming contradiction was the beginning of critical consciousness. Freire distinguishes this conscientization model of learning from the "banking" model in which the teacher attempts to impart his or her knowledge and expertise to the student. In contrast, Freire describes his approach as a "problem-posing" method of education in which teachers and students alike are learners—learning to name the contradictions in their social reality and, by so doing, to develop both a more critical understanding and a greater capacity for social transformation.[1]

The dynamics of developing critical consciousness in the face of contradiction, I want to suggest, motivates learning in two directions at once—inwardly and outwardly. It motivates learning inwardly as the learner is further empowered in his or her own developing capacities. As important, it motivates learning outwardly by fostering understanding about the real contradictions confronting people struggling with oppression in society. Practical theology continues to need such a methodology—an approach to understanding the contradictions we face so that we understand these contradictory social dynamics more realistically and understand ourselves more authentically as we engage these social dynamics. This chapter will attend to corrective methods of reflective practice, which help the leader to understand himself or herself more authentically as a person and as a professional engaged in ministry with others. The chapters that follow will then attend to implications for social analysis as we seek to lead congregations to minister faithfully within an increasingly complex and challenging society.

Before proceeding, however, an anecdote is in order. I had been teaching Bible studies in congregations for years before my spouse, who attended

---

1. Freire, *Pedagogy of the Oppressed*; according to Ramos, the translator, for Freire, "'contradiction' denotes the dialectical conflict between opposing social forces" (28n2).

many of these Bible studies, helped me to understand the importance of attending to contradiction. "You know," she said, "you always begin a session by asking participants: 'What strikes you as odd in this biblical passage?' In all honesty, I had not noticed that I was consistently doing this. But, in fact, I had been repeatedly introducing a key hermeneutical principle in these study groups. Attend to that which is odd, unusual, striking, contradictory, unexpected. That question will feed insight, and it will have you attending to dimensions of the problem at hand that you might not have otherwise. That which applies here to the interpretation of Scripture also applies to the interpretation of situations. When we ask, what doesn't make sense here? we begin to question our own presumptions and assumptions, and we begin to develop critical insight—whether about a passage of Scripture, a challenge in ministry, a problem in organizational management, or our social situation.

The influential work of Donald Schön and Chris Argyris has proven to be helpful for attending reflectively to oneself as a person and to one's practice as a professional. Their method of reflective practice has been utilized within many professions, including the clergy. In a vein similar to Freire's critique of the banking model of education, Schön voiced criticism of the assumption in professional education that professionals acquire expertise and learn skills that they then put into practice. Instead, Schön considered much of professional practice to involve problem-solving and attending to novel situations for which there is no ready remedy in the professional's tool kit. Observing skillful professionals demonstrating a capacity to be reflective, Schön attempted to make these reflective approaches more explicit.

Jackson Carroll

Interpreting Schön's methodology, Jackson Carroll applies it to pastoral leadership in particular. Referring to this as a "meta-method" for reflective leadership, Carroll approvingly cites Schön in identifying different approaches to problem-solving as "frame experiments." Quoting Schön, Carroll explains:

> Such experiments are the heart of reflective practice. They may be of several kinds: They may simply be *exploratory*, consisting of "probing, playful activity by which we get a feel for things," without any prediction or expectation that they will succeed. They succeed when they "lead to the discovery of something there." There

are also *move-testing experiments*, deliberate actions taken with an end in mind. They succeed when they produce the expected end and fail when they do not. In either case, however, they often produce other unintended consequences, which may be positive or negative. Finally, experiments may be *for the purposes of hypothesis testing*, trying to decide whether one course of action is more effective than another.[2]

These frame experiments vary with regard to whether they are relatively spontaneous and intuitive or more intentional, they vary with regard to the degree that they are explicitly goal directed, and they vary with regard to the direction of the connection between theory and practice—that is, whether the experiment is conducted in practice, leading to revised reflection, or whether it is conceived reflectively, leading to revised practice. In either case, reflection and practice evolve together in ways that take into account and respond to novel situations. Reflection and practice are in a reciprocal relationship that empowers learning and creativity when confronting new challenges.[3]

One quick and easy way to reframe a situation is simply to think about it in terms of the different aspects of ministry that are typically taught as subjects in a theological seminary: e.g. preaching, worship, religious education, Christian ethics, pastoral care, church administration, mission and outreach, and the like. In any given pastoral encounter, in other words, one might ponder a series of questions: How is this an opportunity to proclaim

---

2. Carroll, *As One with Authority*, quoting Schön, *Reflective Practitioner*, 145.

3. "Frame Analysis" is often associated with Erving Goffman, a social theorist and author of an influential book by that title. Neither of the two chief sources cited in this and the following chapter pertaining to "framing," however, cite Goffman directly in this regard.

The authors of *Studying Congregations* (21n21) give credit for introducing the concept of framing for their project to Bolman and Deal, *Reframing Organizations*, 15–16. Bolman and Deal cite Goffman's *Frame Analysis* with particular regard to their discussion of the symbolic frame (267) as well as the idea of managing messes (29), which Carroll also develops in *As One with Authority* (128).

Jackson Carroll quotes Donald A Schön, who in turn cites the field of sociology of knowledge generally and, particularly, Karl Mannheim, an earlier theorist who was influential on Goffman. (Carroll, *As One with Authority*, 129, citing Schön, *Reflective Practitioner*, 145; Schön, *Reflective Practitioner*, 312 citing Mannheim, *Ideology and Utopia*.) Schön writes: "Problem setting is a process in which, interactively, we name the things to which we will attend and frame the context in which we will attend to them (*Reflective Practitioner*, 40). For an interpretation of Goffman that treats frame analysis as defining the determinative aspects of "contexts" on the construction of meaning, see Scheff, *Goffman Unbound!*, ch. 5 "The Structure of Context: Deciphering Frame Analysis," 73–92.

God's grace? How is this an opportunity to worship together? Is this a teachable moment? Is this a time for moral discernment? Is this a plea for pastoral care? Is this an opportunity to reach out into the community in mission or to develop the congregation's social network? Is this an occasion for program development or financial planning? Often I find that students for ministry will perceive a pastoral situation within one particular frame of reference but not another. Even relatively simple scenarios in pastoral ministry, though, can exhibit high levels of complexity.

A pastoral encounter might have ramifications for many areas of church life at once. By intentionally reframing a situation as if it were about each of these areas of theological study or ministry practice, the implications for each such area are allowed to come to the fore. For instance, a conversation with a parishioner about a moral quandary might be interpreted, on one hand, as a plea for pastoral care or, on the other hand, as a problem for ethical consultation. Framing this situation solely as a case of pastoral care might incline one toward the nonjudgmental stance of reflective listening. Framing this same situation as a question about ethical teaching, though, will incline one toward a more explicit conversation concerning the various moral resources of the Christian faith that might have bearing on the problem at hand. The very complexity of pastoral situations lends itself to this process of reframing.

Reframing becomes even more important when the situation in question might elicit the pastor's own defensive tendencies—tendencies that we all have. If frustrations arise in the context of a planning meeting, for instance, the pastor might feel criticized, insecure, or threatened. Reframing the conversation as a case of pastoral care, though, can assist the pastor in listening for clues for requests for help or comfort or assurance. Conversely, there are times when the pastor can reframe a situation of pastoral care to realize the parishioner might be making helpful suggestions for planning church programs. Reframing allows one to reinterpret and to listen in new ways. It allows the pastor to move beyond his or her default mode of ministering to attend to dimensions of the situation that may have been initially unnoticed. Most important, these methods of reframing and reflecting require that the pastor scrutinize her or his own motives; they equip the pastor to better view his or her own cognitions, feelings, and commitments in new ways. Such intentional reframing can open pastoral perspective and pastoral practice beyond the confines of either a dogmatically rigid theory, on one hand, or the limitations of uncritically held assumptions, on the other.

Such reframing of one's own perspective opens us to new possibilities of understanding and of action when confronting problems that initially seem insurmountable. Writing about "the gentle art of reframing" in their influential book titled *Change*, Paul Watzlawick, John H. Weakland, and Richard Fisch explain: "To reframe, then, means to change the conceptual and/or emotional setting or viewpoint in relation to which a situation is experienced and to place it in another frame which fits the 'facts' of the same concrete situation equally well or even better, and thereby changes its entire meaning."[4] It is not the external circumstances of a situation that are changed but our own interpretation of it. Reframing allows us to broaden our perspective and to conceive new options.

Writing about pastoral counseling in particular, Pamela Cooper-White notices that one's unquestioned assumptions and motives can function tacitly and uncritically as a guiding theory for one's pastoral practice—but not always in the most helpful of ways. Cooper-White warns about such uncritical tacit assumptions both for "psychological theory" about human behavior and for "practice theory" guiding pastoral practice. She writes:

> Unarticulated theories, I would argue, can be as harmful to parishioners and patients as rigidly guarded conscious formulations. An unarticulated practice theory might be an unconscious conviction that "it is my job to be nice to everyone." Under the powerful sway of this unarticulated conviction, a therapist might end up avoiding exploring painful material with a patient, steering away from conflicts arising in the therapeutic relationship, fostering emotional dependency, and even crossing boundaries under the rubric of being a "special carer." A corollary psychological theory might be that "all people are essentially good" and if given sufficient nurture will naturally grow toward their highest potential. The pitfalls of this general theory include a failure to examine culturally and socially laden assumptions (including racial and gender constructions) about what constitutes "goodness," resulting in an empathic failure to recognize aspects of the patient's aggression, sexual desire, greed, hunger, fear, or hate.[5]

I would add that this statement pertaining to the therapeutic relationship is generally applicable to pastoral relationships as well. We all carry

---

4. Watzlawick et al., *Change*, 95.
5. Cooper-White, *Braided Selves*, 19–20.

assumptions, which serve both as models of the world and as guides to action. These assumptions can actually narrow our perceptions and our options unless they are opened for further critical reflection.

The greatest challenge for new learning is often that which we already know. We become committed to a particular viewpoint or pattern of behavior, and this very commitment becomes an impediment to further insight or alternate perspectives. This is particularly so when the subject in question is oneself—one's effectiveness in leadership, one's personal integrity, one's expertise or wisdom, one's compassion for others. It is challenging to our egos to have to think differently about ourselves, because we become committed to a particular constellation of virtues as constituent to our very identity. When our experience threatens to contradict our self-image in a way that is particularly important to us, we tend to ignore or diminish the self-contradicting aspects of that experience. We protect ourselves—our perception of ourselves—at the cost of new insight or change.

Farber-Robertson

Anita Farber-Robertson has written a most helpful book for church leaders, taking this particular challenge for reflective practice into account. She writes about being "trapped by virtue" to describe this dynamic of resistance to new learning. Following Chris Argyris and Donald Schön, she distinguishes between "model I social virtues" and "model II social virtues." These two models of self-understanding actually name the same set of virtues but provide alternative understandings for these virtues.[6] She uses the language of "model I" to show how a particular perception of one's virtue can actually become counterproductive, and she uses the language of "model II" to show how one's virtue might be understood in a way that opens further possibilities for better communication, healthier relationships, and personal growth.

As an example, she names some of the virtues to which we commit ourselves as (1) "helpfully support people," (2) "respect people," (3) "be strong," and (4) "maintain integrity." But these same virtues might be understood differently or practiced differently with radically different results in each of the two models. To "helpfully support people," for instance, might mean in model I, offering approval and praise, minimizing disapproval and blame,

---

6. Farber-Robertson, *Learning While Leading*, 14–36; see also Argyris and Schön, *Theory in Practice*, 63–109.

and telling people "what they want to hear." In model II, however, the same virtue of helpfully supporting people might be understood as helping them to become more aware of their own reasoning processes, including gaps and inconsistencies. To "respect people" in model I might entail not challenging other people's processes of reasoning, but in model II it might entail acknowledging that people are actually "capable of and interested in learning." To "be strong" in model I might mean, "to show capacity to hold your position in the face of another's advocacy," but in model II it might mean to temper a high capacity for advocacy of one's own position with a "high capacity for inquiry and vulnerability without feeling threatened." To "maintain integrity" in model I might mean to "stick to your values and principles" without caving in, but in model II integrity might mean to advocate for your point of view "in such a way as to encourage confrontation and inquiry into it." To practice each set of virtues according to the two different models, Farber-Robertson demonstrates, can result in radically different outcomes in one's interactions with others.[7]

Significantly, that which might diminish our effectiveness as leaders and that which might discourage insightful new learning is not an individual's lack of personal virtue; it is a person's commitment to a particular self-perception—holding particular understandings of various virtues. Not everyone is committed to the same set of virtues, but everyone is committed to some self-understanding. Not everyone is equally committed to a self-perception of being "strong," for instance, but a commitment to being vulnerable or sensitive can function in the same way. Any virtue can mask from our own self-awareness those aspects of our own functioning that are inconsistent with that virtue.

On one Sunday morning, for instance, I conducted a site visit to a congregation where one of my students was serving as an intern in ministry. On this occasion, the congregation's pastor, who was her field supervisor, had suddenly become ill and was not able to offer leadership within the worshiping community that morning. This student calmly attended to all the gaps in leadership: coordinating others' efforts in Sunday school, planning and announcing activities for the coming week, and leading in worship to a degree that she had not anticipated beforehand. At every level, she functioned marvelously, and people received her leadership with a calm appreciation. Afterwards, in her seminar group at the seminary, her classmates and I strongly affirmed her leadership on this occasion. But she

---

7. Farber-Robertson, *Learning While Leading*, 18–30.

initially deflected our praise. "Oh, I'm really not a leader," she demurred, "that's not where my strengths lie." When asked where her strengths do lie, she offered that she is more of a people-person who is caring for others and encouraging of them, especially in one-on-one situations or face-to-face. "But that *is* leadership!" the class insisted—especially in this instance. It is indeed how this student expresses her leadership—qualities of leadership that were received by members of the congregation and affirmed by members of her class.

This student was aware that she had strengths for ministry—interpersonal skills in particular—but she was not interpreting these strengths as skills in leadership. For her, leadership was more of a public role and less interpersonal. Her daunting image of leadership would entail such capacities as motivating large crowds. By reframing her understanding of leadership to include interpersonal skills, however, she was also able to reframe her self-understanding as a leader. Her new or emerging model of leadership incorporated this interpersonal dimension so that she understood leadership to include her abilities for interpersonal caring and for encouraging others in their work and worship together.

In this example, the student's reframing of the situation and of her role in that situation was facilitated by direct feedback she was receiving in a seminary class. Such reframing of our own pastoral practice is difficult when we are not enrolled in such a class utilizing this kind of reflective process. One can nonetheless enlist the help of others in reflecting together about ministry. Perhaps one is a member of a group of ministers covenanting together to engage in this kind of reflection, or perhaps one engages another professional as a dialogue partner—a coach or a supervisor or even a therapist. It is possible, though, for one to be one's own dialogue partner, if one is disciplined in reflection.

Farber-Robertson provides a method to help with such disciplined reflection. She suggests writing a verbatim of a situation in ministry. Any attempt to write out in verbatim a situation of ministry, I would add, facilitates the reflective process by taking one's inner memories and feelings about the situation and "objectifying" these inner thoughts and feelings on paper for more deliberate analysis. Most processes of writing such verbatims encourage the expression of both the actual record of interactions and one's own inner feelings that might not have been expressed explicitly in the record. In addition, though, Farber-Robertson urges the use of a third category in writing a verbatim. She suggests constructing a third column that forms a reflective "meta-commentary" on the verbatim itself. Thus, she advocates writing and analyzing the situation of ministry in three columns: (1) the spoken and observable record itself, (2) one's own inner voice or voices as the situation was unfolding (including one's own "thoughts, feelings, ideas, observations and evaluations of what was happening" while one was interacting within the situation), and (3) the reflective meta-commentary that includes the "assumptions, commentary and assessments" that one becomes aware of as motivations and explanations for one's actions and thoughts during the situation. This third column allows for a deepening of awareness as one ponders the situation.[8]

The word AWARE can serve as a helpful acronym for deepening one's awareness and self-reflection as one develops the meta-commentary. William R. Noonan, similarly influenced by Chris Argyris in reflective method, suggests this acronym:

> *A*wareness of your private thinking is the main purpose . . .
>
> *W*eigh the risks and benefits of sharing your [inner voice].
>
> *A*ssumptions that you hold with great certainty about others being the problem and having bad motives decrease the chances of having a productive conversation.
>
> *R*eframe your thinking; assume you are not aware of or do not understand others' motives, reasons, and data.
>
> *E*xplore what it is about you that triggered the thoughts and feelings in your [inner voice].[9]

In particular, one is able to become more aware of points of discrepancy between that which one thinks one is doing and that which one is actually doing.

Following Argyris and Schön, Farber-Robertson describes this awareness as noticing the difference between one's "espoused theory" and one's "theory in use."[10] In short, this distinction is the difference between the ways we actually act (theory in use) and the ways we understand ourselves and justify our actions (espoused theory). There is often a gap between these two, and such a gap can hinder our ability to work with others non-defensively. In fact, Chris Argyris has noticed that while people may hold a wide variety

---

8. Ibid., 89.

9. Noonan, *Discussing the Undiscussable*, 21.

10. Farber-Robertson, *Learning While Leading*, 4–5; see also Argyris and Schön, *Theory in Practice*, 3–62.

of espoused theories and self-perceptions, there is surprising commonality with regard to theory in use. Theories in use tend to be face-saving stances, seeking to avoid embarrassment or psychological threat to oneself.

Cognitive Dissonance

Farber-Robertson appeals to the idea of cognitive dissonance to explain the tendency we all have to be self-deceptive. "Cognitive dissonance" is a psychological theory that describes the human motivation to maintain internal coherence between all of one's feelings and cognitions, including one's self-perception. We seek to avoid an unpleasant sense of "dissonance" that can occur when we discover inconsistencies between our most important commitments, feelings, and thoughts. The desired consonance between our cognitions and feelings, though, is not necessarily a formal rational consistency but a subjective psychological one.[11]

Learning and resistance to learning often proceed together. We use whatever mental categories we already have in order to assimilate new information. At the same time, we tend to defend these old categories of thought and resist revising them. When we eventually realize our old categories can no longer simply assimilate the new data coming our way, then a greater accommodation might occur in our mental categories and in our worldview.[12] This is the logic of "cognitive dissonance."[13] We seek to resolve dissonance in our myriad thoughts, perceptions, feelings, and commitments—both by resisting the implications of new thoughts and by further integrating those new thoughts. We can go in either direction.

Returning to the language of espoused theory and theory in use with this understanding of cognitive dissonance, two aspects of our own functioning are often masked to our consciousness by our "espoused theory." Our espoused theory entails a cognitive commitment to a particular virtuous self-perception; it can therefore mask recognition of our behavior that may be inconsistent with that self-perception. First, as we have so far discussed, it is difficult for us to recognize the ways we might be acting in a

---

11. Aronson, *Social Animal*, 88, 131–38; Festinger, "Cognitive Dissonance," 99–113.

12. The distinction between assimilation and accommodation is actually from Jean Piaget and predates cognitive dissonance theory. See Piaget, *Six Psychological Studies*, 8, cited in Wilcox, *Developmental Journey*, 57; see also Gardner, *Developmental Psychology*, 64.

13. Festinger, "Cognitive Dissonance," 99–113.

manner that is *actually inconsistent* with our best values, virtues, and commitments. Second, *even when we are acting in a manner that is consistent* with that virtuous self-understanding, it is difficult to recognize those occasions in which our supposed virtue might actually be counterproductive to our desired ends. Hence, even with the best of intentions, we can work at cross-purposes with ourselves.

In other words, there are many ways to maintain a comfortable sense of cognitive coherence besides learning new ideas or changing one's mind. We can simply deny data or filter out information that is contrary to our self-perceptions or our cognitive commitments. Another "illogical" strategy is to blame others for our frustrations or to project onto others various motivations as contributing to an unwelcome state of affairs. Both blaming and denying are strategies that allow an individual to maintain an internal sense of coherence with one's virtuous self-perception without having to challenge the truthfulness of one's own assumptions, the legitimacy of one's own commitments, or the efficacy of one's own actions.

Indeed, blaming can be pandemic in situations of ministry, and it can be toxic to the congregational community. Frequently I hear pastors speaking of their congregations as "dysfunctional" or describing individual parishioners as "problems." Parishioners too can sometimes blame their pastors when there is frustration within the congregational community or even when there are personal problems that require pastoral care. It is very difficult for a pastor to listen through the explicit expressions of anger from a parishioner to hear an expressed hope for pastoral help with an unarticulated personal problem. Nevertheless, this counterintuitive response is often what is most needed. These methods of reflective practice and of reframing can help a pastor to reinterpret situations in new ways and to listen with new ears.

The idea of cognitive dissonance provides an elegant theory for attending to the concurrence of both coherence and illogic within the same individuals and being expressed in the same situations. When we notice such illogic or apparent contradictions, we are provided with an opportunity to deepen reflection and to listen more attentively. To blame or to deny in these situations is to curtail that reflection and deepening. Such contradiction—whether in oneself, in others, or simply in the situation—is not an opportunity to blame, in other words, but to understand. The idea of cognitive dissonance lets us see that learning can be both facilitated and frustrated by the same cognitive processes. This insight can give us the patience (and perhaps the compassion) to look more deeply at the frustrating or contradictory aspects of a situation and of the actors in a situation (including ourselves!) in order to deepen understanding.

Ladder of Inference

A related concept developed by Chris Argyris and subsequently applied by Anita Farber-Robertson to church leadership is the idea of the ladder of inference.[14] The ladder of inference is a metaphor for the ways we infer and even impose meaning on the words and actions of others. Each successive rung on this ladder represents an increasing level of inference. At the base of the ladder—the ground upon which it stands—are the actual events and occurrences of our lives. These are already interpreted, however, in that we attend selectively to these events and occurrences. We never simply attend to everything at once; attention is always selective. As I sometimes mention in class, "Everything is data, and everything is meaningless—until we start to attend and to interpret it." "Directly observable data" is the ground upon which the ladder of inference stands, but attending to this data represents the first rung on the ladder.

The next rung up on the ladder (the second rung) are the meanings we attribute to the words spoken; these meanings are usually culturally shaped and may be fairly commonly shared. The third rung up, though, represents the particular meanings we attribute to the things that others are saying or doing; these are meanings brought to the encounter by the individual listener. This third rung can infer another's motives and can be evaluative of these inferred motives. Rarely do we realize without reflection that these inferred motives are actually our own constructions that we bring to the encounter and impose on the other person. The fourth rung on the ladder represents the overall theory that we bring to render coherent the inferences and evaluations we are making and to justify these in our own minds.

In using this ladder as a reflective tool, both Chris Argyris and Anita Farber-Robertson recommend attending more carefully to the "directly observable data." This can provide the best check on one's interpretations of that data and one's inferences about others. Some of the directly observable data would be recorded in Anita Farber-Robertson's first column containing the actual conversation in a pastoral situation. Attending to the directly

---

14. Farber-Robertson, *Learning While Leading*, 47–49; see also Argyris, *Overcoming Organizational Defenses*, 87–89.

observable data serves to ground our reflection and gives us the opportunity for self-correction as well as self-affirmation.

As importantly, though, Farber-Robertson's third column (the metacommentary) in a verbatim allows for an opportunity to gain recognition of the psychological and social dynamics in our own interactions with others. The third column allows us to note intentionally a critical comparison between our recorded speech and action (in the first column) and our remembered thoughts and feelings (in the second column). When we make this intentional comparison, we can be attentive to inconsistencies, incongruities, or contradictions. We can also be attentive to too facile a congruence between the first two columns. Any of these critical perceptions represents the potential opening of our ministry in this situation to deeper reflection and insight.

Conclusion

This chapter has begun to explore methods of reflective practice in order to deepen our understanding of our own ministries and to expand our adaptability for ministry. Increasing skill in reflective practice, we have suggested, allows us more quickly to notice our preferred personal patterns of interaction and to open further options for interpreting and responding to particular situations in ministry. Both Anita Farber-Robertson and Jackson Carroll, we saw, provide resources for engaging in reflective practice in ministry.

Jackson Carroll uses the language of "frame experiments" to describe such reflective practice. In this chapter we have explored two basic approaches to reframing our own leadership. The first set of frames at our disposal is simply the various practices of ministry and the disciplines of theological study that have already been part of our formation and preparation for ministry. These various disciplines and practices can serve as different lenses through which we can view a situation of ministry and consider several options for response.

A second approach to reframing of situations, we have suggested, potentially gives us greater access to our own deeper dispositions for interpretation and action. Reflective leadership, we have been noticing, must take into account the leader's own personal strengths and weaknesses, securities and insecurities, style, vision, and preferences. In this chapter, we have recognized nonrational as well as rational dimensions to our leadership in ministry. All of us are characterized by both openness and defensiveness. To be reflective practitioners, we have affirmed, entails becoming more aware of the various and even contradictory ways that we may seek to preserve our own self-identity and self-perception even as we minister with integrity to others. It is hoped that such reflective practice can lead to greater awareness and adaptability in our leadership and service.

Case for Discussion

My first parish is a case in point. In seminary, I had studied very egalitarian and democratic approaches to church administration. The emphasis then—as it usually is now—was on facilitating processes in which the members of a congregation might participate in every aspect of church planning—from brainstorming hopes and dreams to clarifying a vision to establishing goals and priorities consistent with that vision to concretizing a plan to achieve those goals to working together as teams in implementation of the plan to providing clear pathways for communication of evaluative feedback. As a matter of fact, I still teach this model in my seminary classes. But I was surprised in my first parish in Paterson, New Jersey, when none of this seemed to work. During council meetings, the more I attempted to facilitate a mutually empowering process in which everyone had voice, the more frustrated parishioners seemed to become. Finally, one of the parishioners voiced the tacit consensus of all, saying: "Joe, you're the boss; just tell us what to do!" *I was stunned.*

In terms of social context, Paterson is a postindustrial city. Though the entire city is not working-class, the congregation I served was located in a solidly working-class neighborhood, and it drew from members of the working class throughout the city. I am of a middle-class background. I am used to the language of management, and I am accustomed to participating in decision-making whether in the church or the workplace. For my parishioners, the primary model of leadership had been the shop foreman or the store manager. My behavior confused them. They wanted to go about the business of the church (and it was a very active church): worshiping, studying the Bible, feeding the hungry, clothing the naked, driving the church bus, recycling newspapers in order to fuel the church bus, lay visitation, and many other activities and programs for the sake of Christ and neighbor. They wanted me to set priorities and to coordinate their respective contributions to all these ministries. I was distracting them, however, with so many words and questions. I was disenfranchising them, I was surprised to learn, by my very efforts to involve and empower them.

When I realized their expectations, I shifted my behavior to take those expectations into account. I took more of a management role, owning a greater responsibility for organizing our work together. I still consulted, quite extensively actually, but I did so deliberately—deciding when and with whom it was most important to do so, as much on an individual basis as in any formal process in committee. I realized further that my parishioners truly valued meeting together in committees and in council. The value for them, though, was more immediately in the very being together as a fellowship—to support one another emotionally and spiritually rather than to pursue doggedly a task-driven agenda or a formal planning process. Often, the emotional and spiritual support they gave one another when we met focused on issues in people's lives or in the community beyond the confines of church programming per se. I had inadvertently been taking this important time away from them because of my own preoccupation with the planning process and agenda items. Once I modified my preferred style of leadership to take into account their actual style of working together, our work proceeded much more smoothly—and with a greater sense of spiritual discipleship. I was reminded of something my seminary professor in church administration had said but that I had ignored: "Do you need to have a meeting?" he asked. "If not, do something else."

I needed to reframe my own leadership within this congregation. I am not promoting here a model of church administration that should necessarily be generalized to other situations (though I have since encountered many other situations to which it does apply).[15] In many congregations, the shift might need to be in the reverse direction, toward a greater degree of formality in the proceedings of church meetings.[16] The point that I do hope to make with this illustration, at least the point that I myself learned, is that reflective leadership means learning from one's congregants in a given context and being willing to change one's mind and one's manner of ministering.

---

15. For other historical and contextual reasons, Floyd Massey Jr. and Samuel Berry McKinney make a similar point about strong pastoral leadership in many African American congregations in *Church Administration in the Black Perspective*, 23.

16. Parsons and Leas provide a very helpful tool for assessing contextually the tension within a congregation between tighter and looser styles of organizational life along several dimensions: strategy, authority, process, pastoral leadership, relatedness, lay leadership, and learning in *Understanding Your Congregation as a System*.

Discussion

This case anticipates the content of the next chapter, which is about reframing our perceptions of the congregation as an organization—its structure, culture, and processes—when the congregation itself is the subject of our attention. The case provides a segue to that topic. Placed here at the conclusion of this chapter, however, the more immediate focus is on the writer's reframing of his understanding and assumptions about his own leadership. I have written this autobiographically and in an anecdotal style. I hope that I have revealed enough about my internal processing of this incident to allow it to serve heuristically for examining the categories introduced in the present chapter. Since it is my case, others can only discuss it inferentially, but it should nonetheless provide a common frame of reference for a discussion about reflective practice. It is probably best to spend a sufficient amount of time with each of these questions before proceeding to the next.

1. First, if you have a stepladder, you might try telling this story while moving up and down the ladder according to the degree of inference exhibited in the story. You can do this with an actual ladder, or you might use a two-dimensional depiction or even just a mental image of a ladder.[17]
2. What seems to be my (the author's) espoused theory of leadership in this case?
3. What seems to be my theory in use?
4. Are there shifts of either my espoused theory or theory in use during the course of events depicted? How so?
5. What might you speculate to be my Model I virtues in this case?
6. Is there movement here toward a more open Model II understanding of these virtues? If so, how would you describe them?
7. How might cognitive dissonance be at play here

    a. in resistance to learning?

    b. in learning?

    c. in continued resistance to learning?

---

17. The idea of using a stepladder in class comes from Macleod, "Action Science and Theological Reflection in Community."

PART 1: REFLECTION ON PRACTICE

Exercise

Write your own case using Anita Farber-Robertson's method. Include a first column containing the verbatim of a ministerial encounter you have had, a second column revealing your inner voice at the time (e.g. identifying feelings, thoughts, assumptions, and the like), and a third column involving a meta-commentary in which you analyze your own case. As you work with the meta-commentary, try (a) to be open to attending to possible puzzles or contradictions that you may have exhibited in the case, (b) to challenge your own assumptions and to reframe your understanding of the situation and of the individuals involved in the case (including yourself).

5

Framing and Reframing Congregations as Organizations

How one leads is unavoidably a contextual question. It has to do with the people with whom one is in relationship as much as it has to do with the leader's own personality. It has to do with the culture, values, priorities, needs, and strengths of the community in which one's leadership is nested. Reflective leaders discover these aspects of culture and community as they work with the people who receive them in leadership. Sometimes, as the case discussion in the previous chapter illustrates, the discovery can be counterintuitive to the expectations that one initially brings into a context of ministry.

In the previous chapter, we recognized a nonrational dimension to our leadership in ministry. To be reflective practitioners, we affirmed, entails becoming more aware of the ways—both rational and irrational—that we seek to preserve our self-identity and our self-perception while we minister with others. All of us are characterized by both openness and defensiveness. Increasing skill in reflective practice allows us to notice our personal patterns more quickly in this regard and to open up options for interpreting and responding to situations in ministry. We are then able to relate to others more openly and adaptively and less defensively and protectively. Both Anita Farber-Robertson and Jackson Carroll, we saw, provide resources for engaging in reflective practice in ministry. Jackson Carroll referred to this skill of reflective leadership as conducting "frame experiments" on one's own personal practice as a professional.

Framing and reframing can also allow us to examine the larger congregations and organizations in which we are serving. This chapter reviews some approaches to framing and reframing of congregations as organizations, and it highlights some of the key assumptions that make this a fruitful approach for gaining insight about congregational life. It should come as no surprise that congregations as human organizations—like people themselves—are characterized by nonrational as well as rational aspects of their processes and practices. In recent years, there has been an awakening appreciation for the nonrational dimensions of all organizations and institutions. Organizations can be viewed complexly as human cultures displaying the values of their participants—and not just as organized means for rationally pursuing institutional goals.

Organizations as Cultures

To affirm congregations as "cultures" is to appreciate two aspects of institutional life at once. It is to affirm both (1) the rational and formal structure of institutional life and, equally important, (2) it is to affirm the nonrationality of institutional life among the actual people participating in that organization.

Writing in 1992 about the relevance of organization theory for the study of religion, sociologist Paul J. DiMaggio identified five trends characterizing contemporary organization theory. DiMaggio described the first trend as moving "beyond rationality" for organizations in general. Instead of viewing organizations as "rational, efficient means of pursuing collective ends," this perspective acknowledges the difficulty of coalescing the interests of many individuals. It attends to "garbage-can" decision processes within "organized anarchies." The second trend identified by DiMaggio is also related to nonrationality; it is a shifting view of organizational goals. From this perspective, organizational goals are no longer assumed to be clear and shared guides to action. Rather they might also be interpreted realistically as "ambiguous and contested," as representing environmental factors rather than organizational imperative, or as the consequences of organizational discourse. The third trend identified by DiMaggio emphasizes informal social relationships in organizations rather than formal systems. The fourth trend emphasizes organizational culture rather than organizational structure, and the fifth trend examines organizations as open systems or organizational fields rather than as closed systems. "Taken together,"

DiMaggio argued, these trends "make organization theory more relevant to the study of religion."[1]

With regard to congregations in particular, this attentiveness to organizations as cultures is illustrated by the shift in emphasis between Abingdon Press's earlier *Handbook for Congregational Studies* (1986)[2] and the subsequent *Studying Congregations: A New Handbook* (1998).[3] The latter emphasizes studying the congregation's culture and wider social ecology as well as its formal systems and patterns of organization. Of particular note is the use of frame analysis for attending to combinations of formal and informal processes in congregations.

The editors of *Studying Congregations* attribute their particular methodological use of frames to inspiration from Lee G. Bolman and Terrence E. Deal's *Reframing Organizations*, which was deeply influenced by the same trends and schools of thought described by Paul DiMaggio. Bolman and Deal use the language of "framing"[4] to help organizational leaders develop the mindset they need in order to challenge their own assumptions and to interpret situations within organizations in alternative ways. They define frames as follows: "Frames are both windows on the world and lenses that bring the world into focus. Frames filter out some things while allowing others to pass through easily. Frames help us order experience and decide what to do."[5] Bolman and Deal suggest four frames in particular for viewing organizations and organizational leadership. These are the structural frame, the human resource frame, the political frame, and the symbolic frame.

Each of these four frames, according to Bolman and Deal, represents a different metaphor for describing an organization and has different implications for leadership. The structural frame for leadership attends to the formal structure and process of an organization and seeks to align that formal organizational structure with the stated mission and tasks of the organization so that the organization and its constituent parts work in synch like a well-designed machine. The human resource frame looks at an organization in terms of the people that compose it—much like a family—and

---

1. DiMaggio, *Relevance of Organization Theory to the Study of Religion*, 2–6.
2. Carroll et al., eds., *Handbook for Congregational Studies*.
3. Ammerman et al., eds., *Studying Congregations*.
4. Bolman and Deal, *Reframing Organizations*, 17n1; citing Goffman, *Frame Analysis*, 7–11; Goffman, in turn, credits the idea of framing to Bateson, "Theory of Play and Phantasy."
5. Bolman and Deal, *Reframing Organizations*, 12.

seeks to align the organization to the human needs represented there. A political frame recognizes the realities of power and conflict and seeks to establish a power base from which to be more effective. The symbolic frame acknowledges the cultural meanings, metaphors, and narratives that are carried and displayed in any human organization. Like a carnival, a temple, or a theater, any organization as a cultural institution seeks to create deeper faith, beauty, and meaning. Each of these frames can be applied in any organization in order to yield differing interpretations of the organization and different sets of options for leadership and action.[6] Importantly, this series of frames incorporates nonrational and cultural components of human organizations in our analysis along with more rational ones. The most consistently rational frame is the structural frame, which attends to the logical structure of an organization designed to meet its goals. The other frames, though, include to a greater degree various nonrational dimensions of human life in community: e.g. political networking, cultural display of a community's values, and human hopes and needs. All of these frames help to focus attention on important aspects of human motivation and community life that cannot easily be seen in an organizational flowchart.

Each of these frames can help identify strengths in an organization as well as lacunae or areas of unrealized potential. Speaking of the human resource frame in this regard, for instance, they write:

> "The *human resource frame*, based on ideas from psychology, sees an organization as much like an extended family, inhabited by individuals who have needs, feelings, prejudices, skills, and limitations. They have a great capacity to learn and sometimes an even greater capacity to defend old attitudes and beliefs. From a human resource perspective, the key challenge is to tailor organizations to people—to find a way for individuals to get the job done while feeling good about what they are doing."[7]

A tension is represented in this quotation. The tension is between the last line and the thought immediately preceding it. The last line presents the challenge of tailoring organizations to people, but the immediately preceding observation was that people demonstrate both a "great capacity to learn and sometimes an even greater capacity to defend old attitudes and beliefs." The real challenge for leadership indicated here is not simply a matter of adjusting the organization to its constituents' strengths and weaknesses,

---

6. Ibid., 15.
7. Ibid., 14, citing Waterman, *What America Does Right*.

but rather of helping the organization nurture people's best gifts for service and, correlatively, helping the people themselves utilize their gifts in concert with others. In other words, the challenge is to find ways to align the structural and rational processes of the organization that make it "work" with the cultural and human dimensions that make it "tick."

Case: Making Moves

The Costello parish can be analyzed as an organization with reference to each of Bolman and Deal's frames as briefly described here. The Costello parish, one may recall, was described previously in chapter 1 in the case involving "Turkeys," and one may want to review that basic description. It had a food and clothing ministry with the governing motto, "Feed My Sheep."

As Pastor Bryce continued in ministry at Costello, the congregation's food-and-clothing charity grew considerably. The congregation found itself distributing several thousand meals during some months, in comparison to the few hundred meals they once distributed in a typical month. This growth was largely demand driven, as increasing numbers of people in the surrounding community were experiencing poverty.

Those who contributed to the provision of this service were committed to it. The labor force for this endeavor were almost all volunteers—both from the urban Costello parish and from partner churches in the suburbs. Only the Costello church secretary, the organist, and Pastor Bryce were paid employees in the congregation. The director of the food-and-clothing program was a retired man from a nearby suburb who offered his service as a volunteer. He was zealous for this work—especially the hands-on elements of working with other volunteers and procuring contributions of food and finances to fuel the service. He was in the church building most days to coordinate the operation, and he often visited other congregations on Sundays to develop and reinforce the support network.

Of primary importance for the charitable ministry, though, were the dedicated efforts of some of the poorer members of the Costello parish themselves—mostly women heads-of-household who were also struggling to make ends meet on government assistance. These parishioners formed an important support group for one another. The ministry they provided to others also returned back to them a deep sense of self-worth. Many volunteered every day and referred to their donation of time and energy as "going to work." Suburban partners also played an increasingly important role—not just in providing financial donations but in contributing time to volunteer in the urban mission.

A real fellowship and sense of community developed among all the regular volunteers. Everyone ate together every day at a noontime meal prepared from some of the donated food. The meal served three goals: feeding the people present, demonstrating how to prepare some of the donated food, and forging community among the various volunteers and clients.

Food came from four sources. First, of chief importance were donations of food and funds from individuals and congregations mostly within the suburban network of supporting churches. Second, some supplies, especially dairy products, were provided by the federal government. Third, a regional food bank was a source of food made available largely from the food industry; and, fourth, some businesses in the food industry made food directly available to the Costello parish.

As large as the charitable program was, it was still a program of the small Costello congregation, which numbered approximately two hundred members. It was administered under the oversight of the congregation's administrative council. Few members in the congregation had the expertise or the energy, however, to provide a very rigorous supportive structure of accountability for the director, who was exceptionally energetic and creative in establishing the growing network participating in this charitable work.

The entire program was housed in the single-room basement of the congregation, which was also the venue for Sunday school, weekday Bible study, church meetings, an after-school tutoring program, and the church secretary's office. Even with all of these other activities, the basement was usually filled with food and clothing and people giving and receiving. On one busy day, the secretary became frustrated with the amount of food, clothing, and chaos encroaching into her work space, and quit. The director of the food-and-clothing program, too, often expressed frustration with the confining quarters of the church basement.

Pastor Bryce realized that another arrangement was needed to adequately support this growing ministry that was providing a helpful service to so many. Pastor Bryce was in regular conversation with other clergy serving five congregations of the same denomination within the city of Costello and with their immediate ecclesial superior. None of the five had a charitable program of the same scope as Pastor Bryce's congregation, and the pastors of these congregations often voiced appreciation for the level of charitable outreach provided by this program in the Costello parish. One of the five congregations was very small, in fact, and was preparing to discontinue. Pastor Bryce suggested to these colleagues in ministry that their congregations might form a cooperative ministry to jointly support the food and clothing program and that perhaps it could be housed in the building of the congregation that was disbanding.

The idea was well received, and plans went underway to separately incorporate a not-for-profit that would, hopefully, gain the support of all five congregations. Pastor Bryce and the clergy group consulted with a lawyer and began the process of writing bylaws and articles of incorporation. The clergy group also began conversations with the denomination's conference trustees—a larger body with considerable expertise that, they hoped, would agree to maintain the building of the discontinuing congregation for the dedicated purpose of housing the charitable mission. They also kept in touch with ecclesial superiors who voiced support for this cooperative endeavor.

As plans of the Costello clergy group started to take shape, Pastor Bryce brought the program director on-board with these developments. "I've found you a building!" he announced to his friend, thinking this would be the greatest news in world. Pastor Bryce identified the building that was actually in walking distance from the current location. He mentioned that the other congregations would be supportive and that there was a good possibility the conference trustees could maintain the property for this purpose. On hearing this, though, the director insisted, to the contrary, "No, we won't go; we should remain here." Pastor Bryce was surprised, deflated, and uncertain as to how to proceed.

Case Analysis

One can begin to analyze this case utilizing Bolman and Deal's frames by identifying the various elements of the case that seem most prominent within each of Bolman and Deal's four frames.

1. The *structural frame*, remember, attends to the formal structure and process of organizations, and it seeks to rationally align that formal structure with the organization's purpose and activities. This frame is often how people may be introduced to an organization. The following questions might apply. What is the organizational flowchart? What is the committee

structure? What are the formal lines of authority or chains of command? What are the procedures of accountability? What are the explicit rules (e.g. Robert's Rules of Order) for governing the process? How are the organization's structures and processes codified or documented? What is the organization's stated purpose? Is there a planning process to achieve this purpose? How are program planning and financial planning related? How is coordination achieved? How is this organization structurally related to others?

In the case of the ministry in Costello, what aspects of formal structure and process can you begin to identify from this brief description of the case? What further questions about formal structure and process occur to you as you read this case and think about it? How might you describe perturbed Pastor Bryce's situation in terms of organizational structure and process? Attending still to formal structure and process, what would appear to be possible courses of action open to the pastor and the parish?

2. There are two important aspects of the *human resources frame* represented in the two words "human" and "resources." People bring particular gifts, talents, energies, and resources into any organization and its work. At the same time, people are always infinitely more than the resources they bring for the work at hand. People have their own worth as children of God valued by God. They bring their own journeys of vocational discernment of call and sense of faithfulness in that calling. They also bring their woundedness and regrets. They bring their griefs and their joys. They bring their needs for healing and their abilities to heal. They bring their unique personalities, and together they form a unique community.

Congregations and church organizations are often good at combining these two emphases—the "human" and the "resources." There are various inventories to help people identify and affirm their gifts for ministry. There are many such approaches to "gifts-based ministry" and to "mutual ministry." A comprehensive and very accessible guide to these approaches is provided by Jean Morris Trumbauer.[8] Most congregations, such as that represented in the Costello case, have relatively few employees, but the members themselves give of their time and talent to the ministry of the congregation in its community. Indeed, it is not simply that people volunteer their time to support the church; the people themselves constitute the church and shape its ministry.

---

8. Trumbauer, *Created and Called*.

Both of these aspects of the human resource frame—both the "human" and the "resources"—can be brought to bear on the situation in Costello. First, what are the resources represented by the various individuals and groups described in the case? What are they each able to contribute to the work of the whole? Are there gaps in this constellation of resources that perhaps could be filled through recruitment or training? Are there hints of any untapped resources? How are the resources represented in this case engaged or unengaged, coordinated or dispersed, nurtured or restricted?

Now emphasizing the "human" side of the human resources frame, who are these various people that compose the ministering community in Costello? What seem to be some of their needs, wants, or hopes? What seems to energize them? Why do they do church anyway? Why minister? We cannot read the minds of everyone involved in this case, but some indicators are provided. From this perspective of human resources, how might ministry proceed to be most fulfilling for the people involved—for those providing the service as well as those being served?

3. A *political frame*, we said, recognizes the realities of power and conflict and seeks to establish a power base from which to be more effective. This differs from the structural frame, which takes formal lines of authority at face value. The political frame attends to the patterns of networking between people that tend to give credence or legitimacy to different individuals.

Thinking about the different individuals involved in various forms of leadership in Costello, how do they variously form alliances, communities of support, or bases of power? Do you find potential for networking that could be further developed or better utilized? Are there relationships that might be nurtured toward mutual benefit or to effect change? Does one have to take sides in this kind of scenario? If so, how are these sides drawn? If not, how are bridges built? Again this is not about formal authority so much as it is about how leaders—to whatever degree they may or may not be formally recognized as such—work with others in order to get things accomplished.

4. The *symbolic frame*, to interpret Bolman and Deal's approach, draws from semiology in cultural anthropology, especially performance theory. It attends to the actions of individuals and groups not just as displaying meaning but also as creating meaning. How does the organization create and reinforce meaning in its corporate life? What rituals are evident, and what do they evidence? One key element of the symbolic frame is that there

may be more than one meaning displayed in any activity. Often cultural meaning is complex, and symbolism polyvalent. One way of entering the symbolic frame is to imagine the organization as a play or a performance and to notice the levels of meaning enacted by the cast of characters. This is what is meant by the expression, "thick description" of a cultural performance.[9] In particular, how might we view the situation in Costello through the symbolic frame? How do the participants create meaning for themselves? How do they display meaning for others? What values are demonstrated? Are there competing values—plots and counterplots, melodies and antiphons? Are there homegrown rituals? If so, what is enacted in these rituals, or what is reinforced by them?

Further Discussion

If you have been discussing this case in a group, take the opportunity now to reflect on your group process. Was there overlap between the frames as you discussed them? Did one frame seem to predominate in your discussion? Very often, especially when we are first becoming acquainted with an organization, the structural frame can predominate in our reflections, because it is ostensibly both more visible and rational. We may tend to use it rather than the political frame or the human resource frame when analyzing kinks in the organization's process because of this visibility and rationality. But the other frames, because they attend to less rational dynamics in an organization's life, can actually help explain the often frustrating kinks in an organization's formal structure and process.

On the other hand, as you discussed this case in Costello, the personalities of the cast of characters and their moments of confusion or conflict may have allowed any one of the other frames to come to the fore: the political, the human-resource, or the symbolic. Now take the opportunity to notice how each of these reflective frames opens the situation to new insights and new questions. How do these frames supplement and complement each other? What questions or lacunae left from one frame were answered or filled by another? What new insight do you have about the Costello parish as a result of utilizing all four?

Lee G. Bolman and Terrence E. Deal further note that there needs to be a match between style of leadership and the type of organization—both

---

9. Bolman and Deal, *Reframing Organizations*, 293–308, citing Geertz, *Interpretation of Cultures*; see also Turner, *Dramas, Fields, and Metaphors*.

its formal structure and the pattern of human relationships within the organization. Distinguishing between the human-resource frame and the political frame as ways of interpreting leadership and organizational change, they explain:

> *Are you working from the bottom up?* Restructuring is an option primarily for those in positions of authority. Human resource approaches to organizational improvement—such as training, job enrichment, and participation—need support from the top to be successful. The political frame, in contrast, fits well for making change from the bottom up. Because partisans—bottom-up change agents—rarely have much formal clout, they must find other bases of power.[10]

There is an irony in this insight of Bolman and Deal. The phrase, "human resources," might sound empowering to our ears, and conversely the phrase, "political," might carry Machiavellian overtones for us. But Bolman and Deal notice that a political approach requires skills for negotiation and an ability to work with others that are necessary for accomplishing tasks from the "bottom up." In contrast, the human resource approach, as they describe it, requires authority "from the top" in order to be most effective. Was this kind of irony with regard to leadership apparent in your own frame analysis of the Costello parish or in your discussion of it?

The process of reframing that Bolman and Deal advocate allows a leader to challenge his or her assumptions and preferred tendencies toward leadership. One is then able to adjust one's approach to leadership based on reassessments of the particular situation, the type of organization, one's role within that organization, and the others with whom one is working. Finally now, given your analysis of this case and your deepened reflection, if you were Pastor Bryce or in Pastor Bryce's position, what might you now do in ministry in Costello?

Framing Congregational Leadership

Bolman and Deal's frames represent not so much a typology for describing four different kinds of organizations as a tool for reconceptualizing every organization and broadening our conceptualization of the choices we make as leaders within those organizations. Bolman and Deal are encouraging

---

10. Bolman and Deal, *Reframing Organizations*, 273 (emphasis original).

the development of critical insight for organizational leaders. They write, "In assessing any framework for improving organizations, ask if anything is left out. The frame you don't see could be the one that bites you."[11] Moreover, the methodology of reframing need not be confined to any particular four frames. Any framework of this sort is simply suggestive of an expanded horizon of vistas or perspectives on our situation. Bolman and Deal are interested in the management and leadership of organizations, so they attend to four different schools of thought as frames on that particular subject. Other typologies can also serve as evocative prompts for reframing various aspects of congregational ministry.

The handbook for congregational studies, *Studying Congregations*, presents such an alternative typology. Following Bolman and Deal, the authors and editors of *Studying Congregations* chose to use the language of "framing" for organizing the content of this handbook. However, the frames they use are not the same frames for understanding organizational leadership used by Bolman and Deal. Rather, the frames they use are different perspectives on the complexity of congregations in particular. The frames highlighted in this handbook are (1) an "ecological frame," by which they mean social ecology or the analysis of a congregation's social context; (2) a "culture frame," which attends to the many ways in which a congregation creates and conveys meaning and establishes its cultural identity; (3) a "process frame," which attends both to the formal structure of the congregation as an organization and to the informal processes by which people actually work together; and (4) a "resources frame," which includes the financial and human resources as well as the physical assets of a congregation. These frames serve as "lenses" through which to focus on particular aspects of congregational life.[12]

Because this handbook is written as an introductory text for those studying congregations, its readers do not always fully appreciate the degree to which it integrates the rational and nonrational dimensions and the cultural and organizational dimensions of congregations. In fact, the integration is quite seamless and is evident in each of the handbook's frames. In reverse order, the "resources frame" includes the human dimension of resources (inclusive of those other-than-always-rational aspects identified by Bolman and Deal, such as needs, feelings, prejudices, skills, and limitations) and more rational understandings of resources such as the financial

---

11. Ibid., 277.
12. Ammerman et al., eds., *Studying Congregations*, 13–15.

and physical assets of a congregation. The handbook's process frame includes the more rational organizational dimensions of Bolman and Deal's structural frame as well as the more informal networking dimensions of their political frame; the handbook's process frame attends, in other words, to the way a congregation is supposed to be organized and the way it actually runs. The handbook's culture frame is very similar to Bolman and Deal's symbolic frame, with an emphasis on the ways people organize their life together and thereby display their values and create meaning more broadly. Finally, the handbook's "ecological" frame pertains to social analysis of the wider community surrounding a congregation: this includes relatively rational and quantifiable aspects, such as census data, and more qualitative dimensions, such as the cultural traditions represented within the wider community.

The order in which one utilizes these four different frames is not crucial. One can suggest reasons to begin with each. The "culture frame" makes sense as a point of departure, because it focuses attention on the layers of meaning that are already embedded in the traditions and practices of a congregation or a community. As we have seen, newcomers to a community bring a particular perspective that allows them to perceive aspects of that community's culture in ways that might be taken for granted by cultural insiders. At the same time though, we have noticed that newcomers to a community can also miss obvious meanings that others are able simply to assume in their life together. Especially when one is new to a community, the culture frame will present these opportunities and challenges as a methodological beginning for analysis.

Another logical place to begin would be the "ecological frame," which involves social analysis of the surrounding community. This makes sense as a place of beginning because it provides an opportunity to be aware of one's own social location, and it presents an opportunity to be in solidarity with the struggles of one's neighbors. From a liberationist perspective, one might even argue that this is a necessary point of departure in order for our work to be faithful in the service of social justice. While such social solidarity does make sense as an epistemological beginning from this perspective of a liberationist hermeneutic, it nonetheless requires a rather high level of skill when one is initially being introduced into a community of strangers. It may take a lifetime to achieve true solidarity with others, but the beginning point of that journey is the commitment to do so. The "ecological frame" as social analysis can proceed from such a commitment.

PART 1: REFLECTION ON PRACTICE

The "process frame" might be the easiest beginning point—at least with regard to the formal process. It can be fairly straightforward to view an organizational flowchart, to study its polity, to observe any formal planning process, or to attend to any explicit rules for discussion and decision-making. A particular challenge presented by the process frame, though, pertains to understanding informal processes. Behind the organizational flowchart are real people with their idiosyncrasies—their insecurities as well as their strengths, their defensiveness as well as their cooperation, their needs as well as their contributions.

The more informal aspects of a congregation's process can often remain obscure to us even when we find ourselves immersed in their puzzling dynamics. Indeed, we can find ourselves emotionally enmeshed in these dynamics before we realize it. One of the hazards of the process frame when attending to these informal processes is the temptation to blame. Pastors are seldom simply detached observers of their congregation's informal processes. The temptation that most pastors face when analyzing the informal process of a congregation is to start inadvertently labeling people as allies or as difficult individuals, as team players or as obstructionists, as dependable or as high maintenance. I know one pastor who went so far as to mail out a pastoral letter to the congregation that typified his congregants as sheep and goats on the basis of whether or not he saw them as in agreement with his vision for the church. Labeling and blaming others is counterproductive to team-building and cooperative efforts. It is destructive of community, but we have noticed that pastors can fall into this temptation out of their own anxieties and insecurities about leadership. The reflective practices introduced in the last two chapters can help alleviate this tendency by encouraging greater reflectivity rather than reactivity.

Another set of resources along this line are those informed by "family systems theory," such as that by Ronald Richardson,[13] which seek to nurture our capacity to be less anxious in congregational leadership. Using family systems theory, one can chart the flow of anxious energy within a congregation. Curiously, however, I've found that ministers attempting to use family systems theory to chart the patterns of anxiety in their congregations can sometimes exclude consideration of themselves from the chart. If we are not conceptualizing ourselves operating within our congregation's pattern of anxiety, however, we are probably missing much. The point of such an anxiety-charting exercise is to gain understanding of one's own partici-

---

13. Richardson, *Creating a Healthier Church*.

pation within an anxious system in order to become more appropriately connected with others. It should allow one to be able to deliberate insightfully about one's own interactions. Otherwise we can fall again into the temptation to blame rather than frame.

The "resources frame" provides a particularly advantageous point of beginning for analysis to the degree that it brings a positive perspective on identifying resources. A positive approach to identifying resources looks for assets in the whole community—the congregation and its neighborhood and its wider networks. This approach of asset mapping then seeks to further engage these resources through networking, in order to more fully realize their creative potential together. This approach has its genesis in community development and particularly in the work of The Asset-Based Community Development Institute in the Chicago area.[14] It has subsequently been interpreted for use in congregations.[15] In this approach, we seek to discover or uncover resources and assets that may be typically unrecognized as well as those more easily recognized, such as financial wealth.

For instance, people's relatedness to one another—their natural inclination to talk with their more familiar friends or with trusted companions—might seem from the process frame like an informal process with the potential to subvert the more public formal procedure for decision-making. But from a resource frame, people's relatedness to each other and their networks for communication are assets—resources with the potential for further coordinating and communicating their priorities for life and work. It might present a challenge to leadership to learn how to align the organization's formal process with this informal pattern, but the initial task is simply to identify people's relatedness as an asset and potential resource rather than as a potential problem.

Of course, it is possible from within a resource frame to attend pessimistically to a lack of resources. Many churches do this by focusing attention on a lack of members or a lack of financial giving or a lack of community influence. By attending more positively to the many resources of a community as assets, however, we can more easily resist this tendency to problematize the church's ministry. Too often congregations worry so about the glass being half empty that we can miss the springs flowing nearby or in our very midst. The resource frame should help open our awareness to

---

14. Kretzmann and McKnight, *Building Communities from the Inside Out*.
15. Snow, *Power of Asset Mapping*.

possibilities and opportunities rather than simply to problems and needs. By doing this, most congregations—even stressed congregations—can discover more resources available to them than may first appear to be the case. This approach encourages people to engage one another productively as partners in ministry and as neighbors.

These frames are not mutually exclusive boxes for categorizing observations. They represent, rather, different perspectives that one is able to take on the same organization, the same network of individuals, and the same ministry that they undertake together. Each frame serves to highlight different aspects of the organization and its ministry. Taken together, one is better able to picture the organization as a whole and one's role in it. An example of such integration between these frames can be found in Carl S. Dudley's book, *Community Ministry*. Dudley is one of the coauthors of the *Studying Congregations* Handbook. In *Community Ministry*, he starts with the ecological frame of analyzing the social context. Citing Kretzmann and McKnight with regard to asset mapping, though, he attends positively to the resources in the community and the potential for networking between them. He then moves to examine the congregation within its community—both in terms of its processes for organizing people in ministry, and culturally in terms of the congregation's sense of history and identity.[16]

In addition, a fifth perspective pervades each of the other four frames in *Studying Congregations*; this is a theological perspective that seeks the presence of God in every aspect of congregational life. Jackson W. Carroll, one of the coauthors, writes:

> Where is God present in this congregation's unfolding story? Where is God present in its setting? What constitutes faithfulness for this congregation in this time and place and with the particular resources that are available to it? What is God calling it to be and do in the next act? What theological questions are raised by issues and decisions that the congregation faces? What resources are present in its own story and in the larger religious traditions of which it is a part that can help it to answer these questions?[17]

Subsequent chapters of this book will continue to remind us of this theological dimension and present practical approaches for engaging in theological reflection in the communities we serve.

---

16. Dudley, *Community Ministry*, 27.
17. Carroll, "Leadership and the Study of the Congregation," 168–69.

Exercise: Where Do We Worship and Serve?

Does this chapter stimulate your thinking about your own congregation as an organization? One might pause here to employ frame analysis of the actual places in which we worship or where we minister. Two frameworks have been suggested (three if we include the opening remarks about DiMaggio regarding contemporary organizational theory). One might use either Bolman and Deal's frames or those suggested in *Studying Congregations: A New Handbook*.

Each of these methods—indeed each frame within each method—could conceivably entail never-ending analysis. This analysis is potentially never-ending, since there are always new frames that might be employed as lenses, new observations that might be made, and new data that can be taken into account. The point of this exercise, though, is not to be exhaustive in description and analysis. It is simply to take advantage of each frame to open more of the congregation—or different aspects of the congregation—to our perception. As a more bounded exercise, one might begin simply with one of the frames listed below. A more involved exercise would employ them all. If working in the context of a study group in a church, different individuals in the group might be given responsibility for different frames or for different aspects of these frames.

To use Bolman and Deal's frames, simply apply to one's own congregation the same questions that were asked above with regard to the Costello case. Bolman and Deal's four frames, again, are (a) structural frame, (b) political frame, (c) human resources frame and (d) symbolic frame.

To use the frames in *Studying Congregations: A New Handbook*, the questions below can serve as a guide. The most helpful guide, of course, will be the handbook itself and a website that has been developed to further the work of that handbook.[18] A succinct guide has also been provided by Lee Carroll, who summarizes the handbook's four frames and offers helpful suggestions for utilizing them in the context of a given congregation.[19] These four frames, again, are: (1) ecological frame, (2) culture frame (3) process frame and (4) resources frame.[20]

---

18. http://studyingcongregations.org/.
19. Carroll, "Forming Work of Congregations," 79–89.
20. Ammerman et al., eds., *Studying Congregations*, 13–15.

Part 1: Reflection on Practice

Process Frame

For ease of entry, let's begin with the process frame, starting with the formal process. Formal process and procedure will often be written down or formalized in some way. Can you draw an organizational flowchart? What are the different committees and agencies in this congregation or organization? How are they formally connected with one another? What is the official decision-making process for the organization? Are there official rules or procedures for debate? What are the lines of accountability? What are the lines of authority? Is there a formal planning process? If so, how is program planning related to financial planning? Is there an overall strategic plan? Is there a mission statement?

Now as a way of beginning to describe the informal process of the congregation or organization, look back over your observations of the formal process. How does it really work? Who talks to whom? Are the same people on all the key committees, or is the membership on committees more dispersed? What is the relationship between formal authority and the actual power to influence decisions? Do some have more clout than others apart from the formal process? How is conflict handled, or is it avoided? Notice, too, how the congregation or organizational system responds to stress or anxiety. During a crisis, is there a default mode of interaction that takes place that seems disengaged from the formal process?

In short, what seem to be the places of inconsistency as well as consistency between the formal and informal processes of this organization? How do you in particular relate to others within both the formal and informal processes?

Ecological Frame

While the word *ecology* usually refers to systems of relatedness in the natural world, *Studying Congregations: A New Handbook* uses the phrase "ecological frame" more generally to refer to analyzing a congregation within its larger context and, in particular, within its social context. This is not to diminish the importance of the congregation's ecological relationships with the natural environment. There are multiple contexts that shape congregational life. More will be said in subsequent chapters, but a point of beginning is simply to notice and name these different contexts surrounding a congregation. They might include:

a. the natural world, including both living ecosystems and natural services such as the availability of water, air and energy;

b. the local community or neighborhood environing the congregation. Who lives or works here, and how might they be described in terms of economic class, racial or cultural heritage, age, or other demographic characteristics? What histories of inequality or continuing inequality do people struggle with? What industries are here, or how do people earn their living? What is the governing structure of this community? What civic institutions or local associations are there? Is there social change occurring?

c. the global community, which also shapes congregational life. How does this congregation or its local community participate in globalizing forces? How does the international flow of capital or of labor or of goods or of services affect life in this community? How are people being empowered locally to participate in these globalizing trends, and how are they being disempowered?

Resources Frame

One can begin to identify resources either within the congregation or within the surrounding neighborhood. In either case, the intent is to notice the assets that all groups of constituents bring to the community as a whole, even if these assets are currently underutilized. In other words, try to notice the resources of men and women, youth and adults, rich and poor—both in the congregation and in the surrounding community.

First, identify the different kinds of resources present to your *congregation*. The list might include:

- Financial resources—whether of the congregation itself, its individual members, or its wider network of support;
- People's gifts for ministry—from both clergy and laity—including frequently overlooked gifts such as gifts of vulnerability and spiritual resources;
- Physical resources, such as buildings and grounds;
- Other types of resources.

Second, what are the *community* resources in the area surrounding the congregation and within its social network? You may have already begun to identify various constituents and stakeholders in the surrounding community during your ecological-frame analysis. Kretzmann and McKnight suggest attending to different groups of people and types of organizations in a community:

- Many different people. The list of members of a community depends on the actual residents, but it might include youth, seniors, the otherly abled, those receiving public assistance, artists, employers, and employees. They can all be seen to possess individual capacities. What are those different capacities?
- Local associations and organizations, such as other religious institutions, cultural groups, interest groups, and clubs. Again, what different capacities, resources and assets do these various associations hold?
- Local social institutions, such as parks, libraries, schools, colleges, police, hospitals, and the like;
- Potential Economic Resources—whether established financial institutions such as businesses, alternatives such as credit institutions, or potential assets such as underutilized buildings or unrecycled resources in the waste stream.

If you encounter difficulty identifying the resources of these different groups and stakeholders, realize that the first step—an important one—is simply to notice these different groups and individuals and to wonder about their capacities as potential partners in ministry. This opens the possibility, then, of conversation with them to discover areas of commonality, areas of complementarity, and potentialities for partnership. Indeed, it is this very conversation—the establishing of a relationship between various groups in a community—which unearths the potential of helping one another identify their respective assets. A list of community assets will do little good for a congregation if it simply keeps that list to itself. By developing the communications network between groups, new opportunities are found for partnership and community ministry.

Cultural Frame

What are some of the various ways that people live together, make meaning together, and celebrate their identity? How does a congregation display its culture to outsiders and pass on its culture to insiders? Notice, especially, how meaning is symbolized at various levels of congregational life. You might attend to:

- Rituals and other activities as symbolic enactment—whether formalized in worship or shared more informally as patterns in the office or social hall;
- Physical culture and artifacts. What actual things, in other words, carry significance? How is physical space organized?
- What stories are told, especially about the local community, e.g. memories, histories, myths, and legends?

When you look at the congregation as culture from these various facets, do you notice any interesting complexities?

How does the congregational culture seem to compare with the surrounding culture or cultures? A key interpretive question in the cultural frame is, who are we? and, conversely, who aren't we? If the congregation has a mission statement, it is sometimes instructive to compare that explicit self-description of the organization's identity and purpose with the actual ways it symbolically displays and enacts its self-identity in its life and mission. In what ways does the congregation identify itself with the surrounding culture or cultures, and in what ways does it distance or distinguish itself?

PART 2

Methodological Movements

6

Theology in Church and Society

THIS BOOK BEGAN BY asserting two dialectical tensions which would provide the overall conceptual structure for this book in practical theology. The first, you might recall, is the relationship between the community of faith, on one hand, and the wider surrounding community of the larger social world, on the other. The second dialectical tension is the relationship between reflection and practice. So far, the preceding chapters have focused primarily on this second dialectical relationship, providing frames for reflecting on various aspects of practice. To reflect on practice, we have been noticing, is to attend to various levels of community—from individual action to political praxis. We might reflect on personal practices, interpersonal interactions, community organizations, social institutions, or wider social forces—even globalizing trends. We can present this dialectical relationship, complex though it is, as a simple one-dimensional schema:

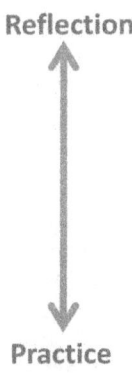

Part 2: Methodological Movements

But how is this reflection "theological"? We have affirmed a theological frame or perspective that seeks to discern and describe the presence of God in every aspect of our common life. This chapter now returns to attend more explicitly to the first dialectical relationship mentioned at the outset—that between the community of faith and the wider social world.

Especially with regard to explicitly theological reflection on practice, we have to acknowledge that theology as "God-talk" occurs within particular communities of faith and that it is shaped in relationship to the practices of these communities of faith. Our communities of faith, in turn, relate to a wider society and a wider world with many diverse people organized in many diverse ways. These people may or may not share our faith commitments and religious assumptions. Conversely, an explicitly religious community may or may not share many of the political commitments and social values common in the wider society. The question is always to be asked, though: in what ways does our religious community relate to the wider social world of which we are a part? This question presents a different dialectical dimension that can be schematized:

In shorthand, we sometimes refer to this question as the relationship between religion and society or between the church and the "world." This is not to imply an absolute distinction between the two. Far from it! Rather, we are simply positing the question of how the two might be related at any given time and in any given place. So, placing these two directions of inquiry together, our schema becomes multidimensional, e.g. for Christian communities:

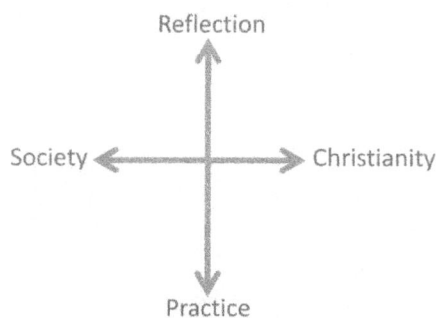

With this conceptualization, reflection on practice is thoroughly social. It is no longer simply "thinking about what I am doing in light of what I believe," or "thinking about what I believe in light of what I am doing." Rather, it is to think about how we as a people of faith are organizing ourselves to relate to the rest of society in ministry or witness. It is to ask, as well, how our very religious beliefs are shaped by and give shape to ideas and ideologies circulating in our larger society.

Each quadrant of this schema represents a different aspect of this relationship. If we begin in the lower-left quadrant, this simply represents our actual life together in society. This is our social praxis, our social location—who we are as social beings economically and politically. This quadrant represents the myriad social forces that make us who we are. When we enter a community, we find people already there, already organized. We find institutions already at work. To begin in this quadrant is to insert ourselves into a community; it is to enter into solidarity with the people already living there. It is to start to live together and to struggle together within the same set of social conditions. These conditions both unite and divide us. These realities of life together in society are represented by this lower-left quadrant.

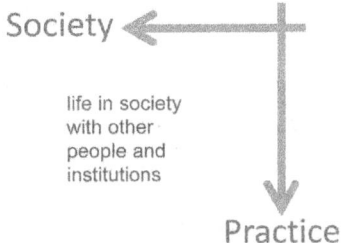

To begin theological reflection here is simply to enter a community. It is not to enter a congregation alone but to recognize that the congregation itself is nested within a larger community and shaped by surrounding social forces.

The upper-left quadrant is what we *think* about life together in society. These thoughts about our social praxis can be either at the level of assumption or deliberation. When we think deliberately and reflectively about our social praxis, we engage in social and cultural analysis. But there are many ideologies as well as analyses competing for people's attention, often assumed—all of them offering portrayals, models, explanations, or even justifications of the social forces at work in the social world. To reflect at this level is to take seriously our lived realities in community. We reflect on social organization and practice within a shared society. We dig deeper to discover political power, economic forces, cultural patterns, institutional arrangements, and the like. We are able to map these social forces in the social communities surrounding our places of ministry. We can give attention to community problems and social struggles on one hand, and to community assets and social resources on the other hand. We can identify both formal structures of political and economic power and grassroots patterns of leadership and authority.

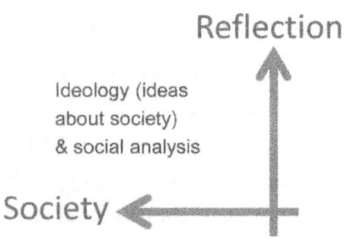

As a particular people of faith, moreover, how do our religious beliefs and assumptions reflect other important patterns of thought and ideologies in our shared social world? How can our theological reflection be informed more deliberately by our own social analysis? How might our religious thinking enrich the larger shared world of meaning in our common culture? These are questions that move us into the upper-right quadrant.

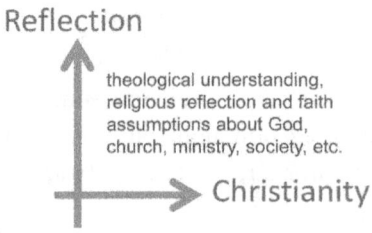

Our explicitly theological reflection points our attention toward God and to divine realities. But at the same time we continue to attend both to our shared world of meaning in society (represented by the upper-left quadrant) and to our own practices in ministry as people of faith (represented by the lower-right quadrant). By engaging in explicit theological reflection, we hope to unite the two more deliberately—to relate our own religious practice faithfully and meaningfully within a larger world of social meaning and cultural understanding.

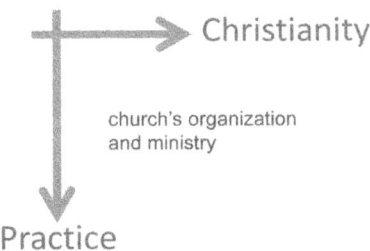

The lower-right quadrant represents our particular practice as Christians organized in whatever form. Our practice as Christians is the concrete reality of our life together in this world. It includes the institutional and social form of our church organization, the actual practices of ministry by both clergy and laity in church and society, and the many ways we may seek to serve our neighbors in the wider society—whether through service, evangelism, advocacy, or social action. Our practice as Christians also includes ways we might want to distinguish ourselves or to separate from the larger society, and it includes ways we might cooperate with—or even be co-opted by—others in society, such as in service of war or wealth. It represents whatever we do as Christians and however we are organized. We hope that our ministry, our practice, as Christians (represented by the lower- right quadrant) will be consistent both with our most faithful theological understandings (represented by the upper right quadrant) and with our most loving and just engagement in society (represented by the lower left quadrant).

We are challenged to make these connections. We are all engaged in the practice of ministry. Theological reflection on this ministry is a part of "practical theology." The ministry itself provides the primary data for theological reflection. Moreover, our ministry occurs in cooperation and in concert with each other. We work together in ministry within particular contexts of service. Our learning partners are our fellow laborers—clergy and lay. We can reflect together about the nature of our work as ministry in service of both God and neighbor. We reflect together in order to make these connections more visible, even as we work together to make our ministry more effective. We are aiming to be faithful in both our practice and our reflection—and both individually as faithful followers and collaboratively in faithful fellowship.

For people just starting to minister in a particular congregation, this fourth quadrant on the lower right is actually their beginning—their point of departure for practical theological reflection. They begin the process by entering a place of ministry and by engaging in that ministry. This point of entry—actual engagement in ministry—provides an opportunity to do socially relevant ministry and to do faithful theological reflection. But it also presents challenges.

One challenge is simply to engage theology deliberately and reflectively while engaged in the busy practice of ministry. How do we make the connections between our own ministry and the resources of the faith? Notice that this challenge is all on the right side of our grid—that concerning religious reflection on religious service and involvement in church practices. How do we reflect theologically on our own experience of ministry in a largely religious context?

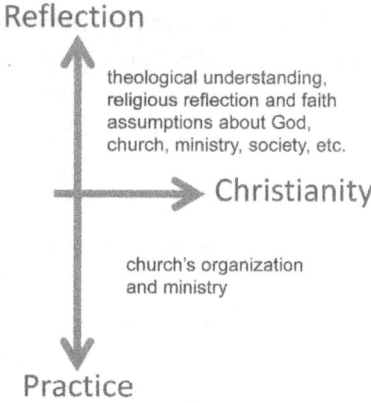

Another challenge we face is to steer our own ministry and to steer the religious organization's practice into relevant connection with its surrounding community and with the larger society. How does our practice as Christians actually relate to the realities our neighbors face? This challenge is all on the lower half of the grid—that concerning ministry as concrete engagement with others in society.

Theology in Church and Society

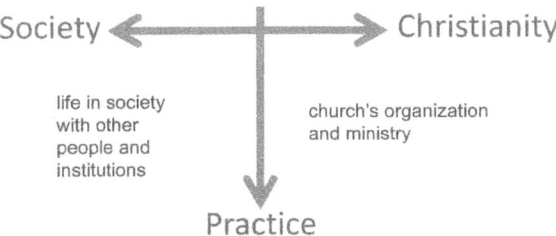

A compound challenge is presented, though, as we seek to be engaged in each of the four quadrants that we have described—to be engaged both practically and reflectively in both church and society. We can become so busy in community ministry that it takes energy to move into a reflective mode and to access the resources of our faith. Conversely, we can become so occupied and even preoccupied with our religious context—both our practices of ministry and our theological reflection on ministry—that we find ourselves (and find our congregations!) disengaged from the social life and the social problems surrounding us.

Several methods of theological reflection can be seen to cycle us through each of these quadrants successively. These can be grouped into families, but they all tend to have in common this circular movement through these four quadrants. These methodologies include the liberationist hermeneutical circle, the pastoral cycle, contextual theologies, and methods of practical theology. These all tend to:

(a) begin with experience in society,

(b) move to deepen our critical understanding of our social experience,

(c) engage in explicitly theological reflection on this deepening understanding,

(d) inform the church's ministerial practice, and

(e) move that ministerial practice toward effective engagement in society.

All of these methodologies tend to have in common a version of this cyclical theological method that incorporates reflection on practice in church and society.

PART 2: METHODOLOGICAL MOVEMENTS

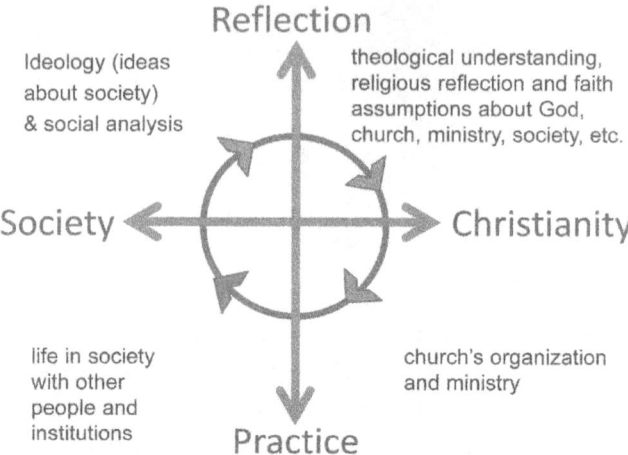

This method can be used descriptively, reflexively, or constructively. Descriptive and reflexive uses will be described below and utilized in the concluding exercises of this chapter. The following chapter will then further explore a constructive use of this method.

A *descriptive* use of this method allows us to analyze a ministerial practice or a theological statement contextually. For any given ministerial practice or for any given theological statement, a series of four questions (or four groups of questions) can be asked:

1. What is the social location of the practice of ministry, of the practitioner, of the theological utterance, or of the speaker? How might this social location or social context have shaped the practice of ministry or of the expression of theology? (lower-left quadrant)

2. How might we understand this social context better? What social forces are at work? What divides or unites people in this social context? What are their struggles? What are their victories? How do they understand their own social situation? How, then, does this practice of ministry or this expression of theology reflect these social conditions, address these social issues, or confront these social dynamics? (upper-left quadrant)

3. What are the explicitly theological resources being accessed in this practice of ministry or expression of theology? What religious symbols are employed? What aspects of the tradition are highlighted? What parts of Scripture are read? Conversely, what is omitted? How

do these theological ideas reflect or confront (or reflect *and* confront) ideologies and values within the wider social context? (upper-right quadrant)

4. How is this expression of theology reflected in practices of ministry or, conversely, how is this practice of ministry indicative of a particular theological perspective? Is this practice of ministry engaging mostly church people, or does it reach into the surrounding community? How does this practice of ministry continue a tradition? How does it alter tradition? How does this practice of ministry reflect social realities? How is it hoped to transform social realities? (lower-right quadrant).

Exercises for Reflection

Use this method to analyze a theological book, essay, or sermon. If you are conducting this exercise in a group, you might want to choose to analyze theological material which the whole group is reading. If so, it would be most instructive for participants to analyze the material independently from one another before comparing notes about their respective analyses. The purpose of this exercise is not to discover whether or not participants agree with or like the material in question. It is rather to help participants to better appreciate the relationship of the theological material to its social context and to the church's praxis.

1. As a first step, you might begin by drawing the methodological grid on a sheet of paper (see diagram below) and then, guided by the above questions, making notes in the relevant quadrants.

2. Second, after having mapped the theological material in the relevant quadrants of the grid, notice how the different quadrants are conceptually connected. For instance, between the upper two quadrants you might ask, what ideas about society invoke or inform what theological affirmations? Here you are looking for "bridge notions" between the two quadrants that connect the writer's thinking about society with his/her explicitly theological reflection.

3. Third, you can then proceed with interpreting your map of this theologian's ideas in a brief essay, showing the connections as we cycle through the four quadrants, between social context, understanding of society, theological articulation, and implications for ministry.

PART 2: METHODOLOGICAL MOVEMENTS

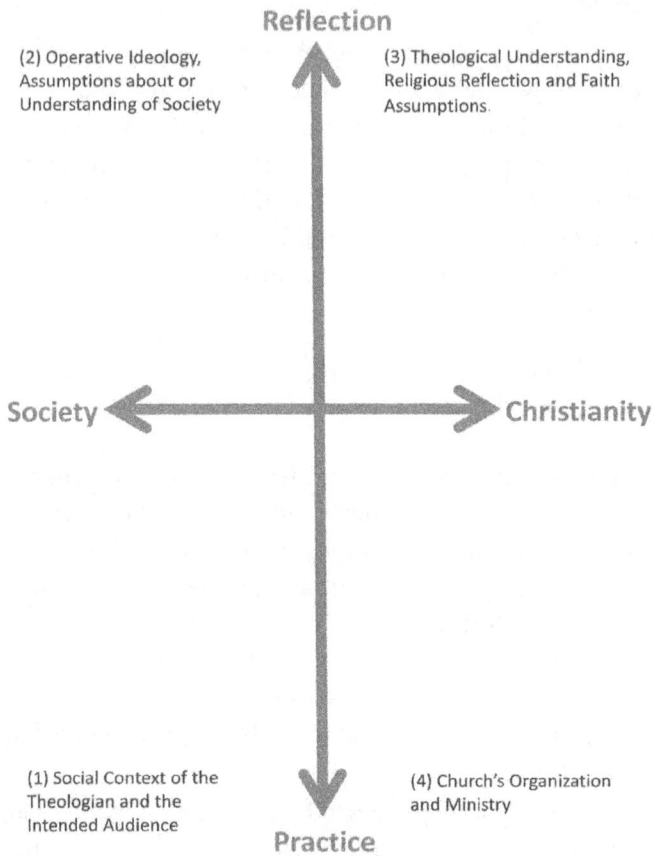

Exercise: Reflexive Use

Use this method *reflexively* to analyze one's own theology. Using the same grid and set of questions, you can choose to analyze any essay you've written or sermon you've preached. Also, a reflexive use of this method can raise these same questions about your practice in ministry. As above, first use the grid to chart your social context, understanding of society, theological ideas, and engagement in ministry. Then, second, look for the connections between these four areas. This can be done alone or in a community of learning or a community of practice. It can be instructive to do this exercise together with others as conversation partners.

This reflexive work can be quite difficult. A reflexive use of this method and of this grid helps us to understand our own theological affirmations better. It helps us to see the ways in which our theology might reflect our own social location. It helps us to appreciate the ways in which our ministry might reflect our theology, and the ways in which it might not. The temptation in using this method reflexively, though, is that we might want to emphasize a more logical coherence between the quadrants than is actually reflected in our faith and work. Similarly, we might want to ignore or gloss over areas of disconnect or contradiction between the quadrants when examining our own thought and practice. The value of this method reflexively, however, is that it allows us to reach a greater appreciation of our own theological thought and praxis (perhaps even at the level of assumption) with regard to both consistency and inconsistency as they become apparent to us in the process. Nevertheless, in using this method reflexively, we might decide to aim at a greater degree of coherence in our theological thinking, our ministry, and our social praxis. To do so moves us into a constructive use of this method, which is the topic of the next chapter.

7

A Constructive Approach

IN THE PREVIOUS CHAPTER, we identified two dialectical dimensions or tensions giving shape to practical theology. In addition to the dialectical relationship between reflection and practice, we affirmed a dialectical relationship between Christian praxis and the praxis of the wider society. We found that these two dialectical relationships can be conceptualized as a matrix. The matrix forms a grid with four quadrants that allow us to ponder sequentially and in relation to one another: (1) our location in society, (2) our thinking about society, (3) our theological affirmations, and (4) our engagement in ministry. Various methods for doing theology can be seen to navigate movement through each of these quadrants. We will compare some of these methods in the following three chapters. These methods include a pastoral cycle, a hermeneutical circle, and the cyclical method of practical theology.

We have already noticed how this basic methodology can be used descriptively in analyzing any expression of theology with reference to its connection to social ideology on one hand and to the church's practice on the other. We noticed as well that this same methodology can be used as a reflexive tool to better understand one's own theology and ministerial practice in society. This reflexivity moves us now toward a more intentionally constructive use of this method.

A *constructive* use of the methodological circle seeks to articulate a theology that is relevant to our practice in church or society, or it attempts to develop ministerial practice in a direction that is more socially relevant or theologically informed. A constructive use of this method might begin

A Constructive Approach

in any of the four quadrants and explore the connections with the adjacent quadrants. But very frequently one is advised to begin with the social situation itself, which is represented in the lower-left quadrant. This point of entry allows one to begin to take the perspective of people in a neighborhood or local community. Proceeding through the quadrants around the methodological circle, then, we would ask the following.

1. How do we enter a new community, or how do we enter into solidarity with the marginalized in a community, or how do we take our own social context or social location seriously? These are questions that simply situate ourselves initially within a social context.

2. From there we move to analyze the social forces at work in this social context—whether economic, political, cultural, ideological, or related to family structure. We can explore patterns of oppression such as racism, classism, and sexism. We can examine historical patterns that have shaped this community, such as slavery or colonization or evangelization or capital investment or warfare or immigration or globalization. We look for connections between these social forces. This is the intellectual work represented in the upper-left quadrant; we reflect deliberately on the dynamics of our social praxis.

3. Explicit theological reflection, then, attempts to make connections between our reflection so far with our religious faith—its sources and symbols, its historical traditions and its contemporary breadth. What might our theological heritage have to say to our social situation as we have analyzed it? Correlatively, what challenges or questions or insights does our social analysis present to our theological perspective? Sometimes our point of access from the social to the theological is a quandary; sometimes it is an insight.

4. Finally, then, how does our theological exploration in light of our social analysis move us in thinking about ministry? In what ways might we need to change or to persevere? How might we need to sever ties or build alliances? How might we need to deepen our own spiritual practices or expand our social outreach? How might the laity be involved as well as the clergy, or how might the community be involved as well as the congregation? And, indeed, how do we expect or hope this emerging ministry to affect or even to transform the real lives of neighbors in shared community?

Part 2: Methodological Movements

Methodologically, we focus on each set of questions as represented by the respective quadrants. But then we also need to attend to the possible connections between each set of questions. What theological ideas make connection with cultural thinking? What theological ideas might inform new ministerial practices? What congregational practices might connect with social movements for change? We need to look for bridge notions and bridge practices between each of these quadrants. So, our schema might now look like this:

As we embrace this method and start to apply it constructively, however, we frequently encounter a divide rather than a connection between each of these quadrants. It may be that no one set of questions seems to lead automatically to the next set of questions. There is no logic of necessity between one set and the next. The movement from one set of questions to the next—or between one quadrant and the next—requires intuitive jumps or imaginative associations as much as logical connection. For the method to work meaningfully, though, these connections need to be made. Between adjacent quadrants there must be a bridge to guide our reflection or to channel our action.

A Constructive Approach

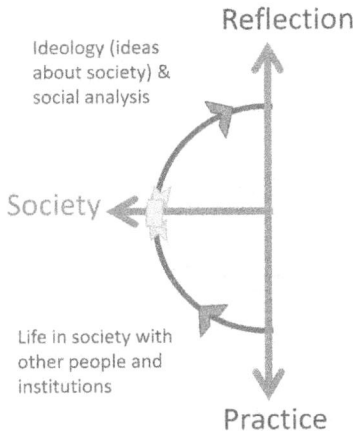

In making the initial move from our basic experience of life in society to critical social analysis (that is, from the lower-left to the upper-left quadrant), there are different possible points of departure. One way is to cast the net broadly, looking at the social context from various angles and perspectives. Joe Holland and Peter Henriot emphasize the importance of social analysis for the Pastoral Circle.[1] They suggest ten questions that can be used by any group seeking to understand their local community or neighborhood more clearly:

1. What do you notice about our situation here today? What are people experiencing?
2. What changes have occurred in the past twenty years? What have been the most important events?
3. What influence does money have in our situation? Why?
4. Who makes the most important decisions around here? Why?
5. What are the most important relationships people have here? Why?
6. What are the most important traditions of the people? Why?
7. What do people want most in life? Why?
8. What will things be like in ten years if they keep going in the same way? Why?

---

1. Holland and Henriot, *Social Analysis*, 8. "Pastoral Circle" and "Center of Concern" are trademarks of Center of Concern (www.coc.org).

Part 2: Methodological Movements

9. What are the most important causes of the way things are today? Why?

10. What did you learn from all of this?[2]

These questions are simply put, but they cover a lot of territory. In fact, each question is a way of reframing one's understanding of the neighborhood or local community. Questions 2 through 6 seem to invoke broad disciplinary areas of the social sciences, but in language accessible to anyone regardless of educational level. Indeed, this method is well suited for use by congregational study groups. Historical analysis is begun with the question about changes and events in the past twenty years. Economic analysis proceeds with the question about the influence of money. Political science is touched when we ask, who makes the most important decisions? Sociology and cultural anthropology deal with the importance of relationships and traditions.

All these questions help to address the so-called ecological frame as described in the *Studying Congregations* handbook discussed above in chapter 5.[3] But, also as suggested there, we might want to add a question or questions dealing specifically with ecological relationships in the natural environment. In his encyclical letter, *Laudato Sí, On Care for Our Common Home*, Pope Francis emphasizes the importance of integrating environmental and social analysis. He writes:

> it is no longer possible to find a specific, discrete answer for each part of the problem. It is essential to seek comprehensive solutions which consider the interactions within natural systems themselves and with social systems. We are faced not with two separate crises, one environmental and the other social, but rather with one complex crisis which is both social and environmental. Strategies for a solution demand an integrated approach to combating poverty, restoring dignity to the excluded, and at the same time protecting nature.[4]

We should therefore include ecological questions about the natural environment along with the other questions for social analysis enumerated above, questions such as:

---

2. Ibid., 102.
3. Ammerman et al., eds., *Studying Congregations*, 13–15.
4. Francis, *Laudato Sí*, (139).

A Constructive Approach

11. How are environmental services, such as clean water or air, apportioned, protected, or degraded?
12. How is societal activity related to the life and health of plants and animals in the area?
13. What are the sources and uses of energy, and is this use sustainable?

When we add these ecological questions to the others regarding analysis of society, we see that this approach is truly multifaceted. The bridge between our experience of a social context and our deepening understanding of social realities is presented here as a broad passage, like a multilane highway, guiding us between the two quadrants.

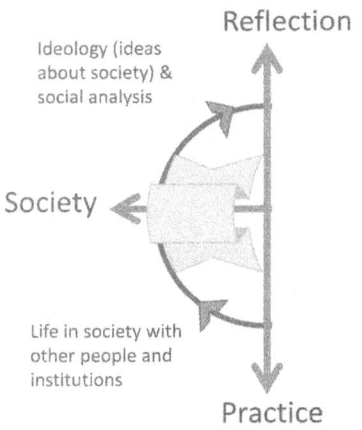

If this seems so broad that one is unsure where to begin, there are several ways of focusing attention more precisely. One way is simply to pick any one of these questions and to begin there—even if that choice seems to be an arbitrary one. Social conditions tend to overlap, and social forces tend to collude. If one begins analysis of a community with any particular focus in mind—whether it is economic influence or political structure or a community's history or patterns of racism or gender analysis—one is likely to soon encounter these other areas as well. To begin analysis anywhere is to open our experience to a deepening understanding and a broadening perspective.

Another way to focus attention is to attend intentionally to the perception of any problem being faced by a community. Holland and Henriot's approach to social analysis is designed to help a group of people identify problems being confronted in a local community, and deepen that group's understanding of the causes of such problems. Their ninth question asks specifically about these causes. One way of focusing attention is to align with people's perception of the problems they are facing as a community. Their experience of these problems or their struggle against these problems may suggest natural points of engagement for further analysis. In fact, their experience may impel the analysis. For instance if people are hungry, one might ask why it is that some people have less than is sufficient while some have more than enough. Our very experience of a problem can determine the next line of inquiry. The identified problem, then, provides the bridge from experience to social analysis of the forces that might be causing or aggravating that problematic social condition.

In a similar vein, we have already noticed that contradiction can stimulate critical reflection. Any perception of counterbalancing forces in society, or recognition that our experience may not be consistent with cultural myths or political ideologies, or simply the suspicion that things are not always as they appear, can provide the initial insight and incentive for further social analysis. To reiterate, this has been the method employed in this book—to begin reflection with a recognition of our social location and then to notice contradictions that inspire further reflection, whether these be contradictions apparent in our own functioning in ministry or reflected in the wider social dynamics of our communities. In this instance, it is the perception of contradiction that provides the avenue or the bridge to further social analysis.

Finally, while problems need to be addressed, they sometimes can appear overwhelming. We can be discouraged rather than encouraged when naming contradictions or when confronting problems. Another approach is to attend appreciatively to the assets and capacities in a given community. This is not to deny the problems or to ignore the contradictions. It is, though, to attend deliberately from the outset to the resources and potential resources represented in a community. This asset-mapping approach is used in community organization[5] and increasingly in the work of congregations with their neighbors.[6] In this approach, our analysis explores, inventories, and affirms the many different assets that might be present in a community. To do so requires that this analysis proceed in conversation with neighbors and neighboring institutions. We cannot discover one another's assets un-

---

5. Kretzmann and McKnight, *Building Communities from the Inside Out*.
6. Snow, *Power of Asset Mapping*.

less we are communicating. The discovery and naming of our respective assets, then, presents the opportunity for further networking, cooperation and collaboration. This would therefore add yet another question (or other questions!) to those posed by Holland and Henriot; in fact this might be the prior question:

14. What are the various assets, capacities, and resources represented among the diverse people and institutions in a community?

As I explained previously in chapter 5, Kretzmann and McKnight of the Asset-Based Community Development Institute suggest that we identify the various groups of individuals that might inhabit a community (such as youth, seniors, otherly abled people, artists, people on government assistance, and so on) and then explore the capacities they have that might be overlooked or underappreciated. Such capacities would include any and all skills—whether celebrated or marginalized in popular perception, people's networks and relationships in the community, and any "enterprising interests and experience."[7] Similarly, resources are identified pertaining to all local associations, religious groups, cultural organizations, and local institutions (such as parks, libraries, schools, colleges, police, hospitals and health-care services, and the like) Such corporate assets might include land and buildings, financial resources, human resources, organizational skills, experience in providing programs, social networks, and the like. The primary focus throughout is on the local community—its people and its assets. There is still a focus on problem-solving, but with an eye to the opportunities for collaboration between groups, networking in new ways, and the creative and constructive use of a community's capacities and resources. The methodological bridge between the experience of life in a community and an asset-based analysis of that community would be the very act of social networking with an eye toward discovering the capacities held by members of that community.

Any of these facets, though, might provide for a bridge between our basic experience in community and our social analysis of that community: problem perception, awareness of contradiction, openness to capacity. With our attention focused in any of these ways, we can proceed to social analysis, making use of either Holland and Henriot's set of questions or

---

7. Kretzmann and McKnight, *Building Communities from the Inside Out*, 15.

Part 2: Methodological Movements

Kretzmann and McKnight's inventory of assets to further our understanding—and our appreciation—of the community.[8]

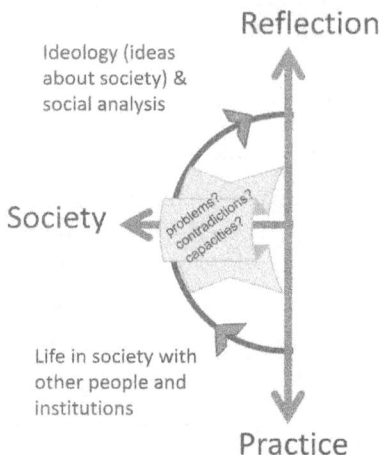

Notice, though, that we are bridging between our shared praxis in community and our analysis of that community (the left side of the grid). We are not attempting to bridge directly from our particular praxis as Christians to social analysis. This is not to deny our Christian identity or our evangelical mission. However, if we seek to shortcut directly from our own programmatic priorities to the analysis of a community, we tend to be more agenda driven. Our questions become these: Where can we find resources for our programming? Where can we find potential converts? Where can we find political allies for our cause? There is nothing necessarily wrong with pursuing these questions, and congregations and other religious organizations may need to do so for the sake of their mission. But it is a one-sided focus that runs the risk of misunderstanding the neighbor, misrepresenting the community, and mistaking self-promotion for mission.

8. The reader may have noticed a similarity between the subject of this chapter pertaining to "social analysis" and that of chapter 5 above pertaining to the "ecological frame" for *Studying Congregations*. In fact they are very similar; both focus attention on the social context, but there is a subtle shift of emphasis. In chapter 5, our attention was focused primarily on "congregations" as the object of our study, and we employed the so-called ecological frame as a way of attending to the congregation's social environment. But the congregation was still of primary concern as the object of analysis. Social analysis in chapter 5 provided an "ecological frame" on the congregation. Here, now, the congregation is represented not so much as the object of our study, but agenticly as the one engaging collaboratively in research of its shared neighborhood and seeking to form more meaningful alliances with its neighbors.

A Constructive Approach

That which we are advocating instead is to begin in solidarity with one's neighbors—already to see one's neighbors as beloved of God. To the degree that we can live in solidarity with our neighbors in a community, we are better able to understand the community from their vantage point and to share with them in their struggles, their hopes and disappointments. Solidarity provides the bridge between our particular practice as Christians and our shared practice with neighbors in the wider community. This shared practice, then, gives us a common frame of reference with our neighbors. It allows us to engage in social analysis with our neighbors rather than social analysis of our neighbors.

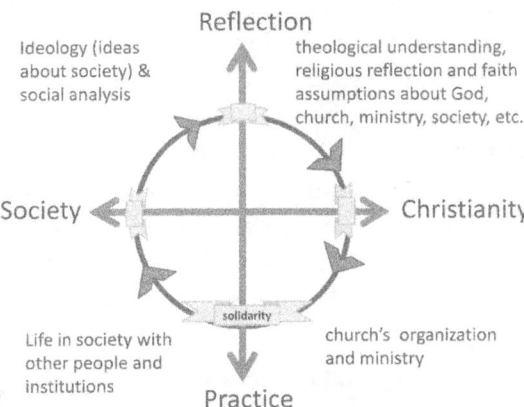

Part 2: Methodological Movements

This rooting of the church's life and ministry within its surrounding society and in solidarity with its neighbors is seen here as a precondition—not just an outcome—of contextualized theological reflection. In his influential book *Constructing Local Theologies*, Robert J. Schreiter writes about such contextual models of doing theology:

> The contextual models, as the name implies, concentrate more directly on the cultural context in which Christianity takes root and receives expression . . . contextual models begin their reflection with the cultural context. Contextual models are seen increasingly as embodying the ideals of what local theology is to be about, even though the working out of those ideals often proves difficult in the practice.[9]

Moreover, the praxeological solidarity that we are advocating does not negate the church's mission but rather informs it. J. Andrew Kirk has noted that such contextualization and inculturation has been an important missiological emphasis since the mid-twentieth century.[10]

Our Christian identity does not exclude our simultaneous identification with our neighbors in other communities. The apostle Paul, for instance, is portrayed in Acts 22 as claiming both his Jewish and his Roman identity sequentially even as he was in the process of communicating the gospel of Christ. For myself, more immediately, I can at once be a Christian and a Marylander; I can support my congregation's ministry along with my fellow congregants at the same time that I support the environmental work of the local Little Falls Watershed Alliance[11] along with my neighbors. I do not cease to be a Christian when I work with my neighbors, and I do not cease to be a neighbor when I go to church. We literally drink the same water.

To reflect further on the importance of, say, water for a particular community will involve us in both contextualized social analysis and contextualized theology. When we allow solidarity with our neighbors to form a bridge between our particular praxis as Christians and our shared praxis in society, we discover the importance of elements such as water for

---

9. Schreiter, *Constructing Local Theologies*, 12.

10. Kirk, *What is Mission?*, 90–91; similarly Luis J. Luzbetak emphasizes the missiological importance of inculturation or contextualization (which he identifies synonymously) especially for the goal of evangelization, in Luzbetak, *Church and Cultures*, 69–73.

11. http://www.lfwa.org/.

A Constructive Approach

our common life together. Water is an element in our shared practice as a community.

Continuing with water as an example, it might seem that water is so prevalent a reality that we can dive immediately into explicit theological reflection about it without the mediation of social analysis, and we can. Theologically, we might understand water relating us to each other in primordial creation, our common experience of birth, our new birth by water and the Spirit.

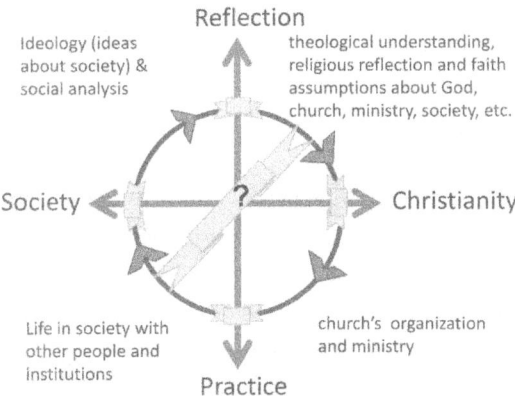

But we then might miss the opportunity to reflect theologically on the particular importance of water for this specific community—whether that be the cleanliness or pollution of water, its abundance or scarcity, its use in agriculture or industry... How do we understand the economics of water, the politics of water, the social history of water in this place? Furthermore, how might we then think theologically given our understanding of these social dynamics involving our common practice in water?

Indeed, because water is so common a reality, it necessarily has its own history within each and every community. If we ignore this social particularity of water, we find ourselves simply talking to ourselves with our own inherited symbolism, preaching to the choir, as it were, rather than joining in the chorus. Let me illustrate with some of my own experiences of water among a variety of communities where I've served.

PART 2: METHODOLOGICAL MOVEMENTS

Reflections in Water: The Aquifer

One day in chapel in a seminary where I taught in the United States, ecologically concerned students and a member of the faculty had decided to lead an environmental worship service focusing on water. They read passages of Scripture and sang hymns with images of water. The sermon emphasized the importance of conserving fresh water and included practical suggestions to avoid wasting water.

None of the students, though, recognized the fact that they were preaching and singing on top of a polluted aquifer that was being cleansed at great public expense as a federal Superfund site. This lack of attention was despite the location of the pumping and cleansing station immediately across the street from the seminary and the presence of monitoring wells all around the neighborhood. A munitions factory in the community's history had allowed organic solvents to leach into the aquifer. The problem was being contained by pumping the polluted water out of the aquifer at a faster rate than it could spread and then using carbon filtration to remove the carcinogenic compounds. This process provided all the drinking water for this municipality—and then some. Because the water had to be pumped from the aquifer and filtered at a fairly fast rate as a matter of pollution control, there was clean water to spare—more than the municipality could use. If neighboring municipalities did not need it, it was simply cleansed and discharged. Preaching conservation in this particular situation seemed to me ironic—well-meaning but misplaced, misinformed due to being decontextualized.

Another group of students and their teacher, however, arranged to take a tour of the Superfund pumping station. Their tour-guide was the chief technician at the pumping station, who gladly and proudly showed them the equipment and explained to them the process. He gave them a history of the cause of the polluted plume of water and of the federally funded technical solution to the problem. The class was most impressed, and the teacher thanked the technician at the end of the tour saying, "This is amazing what you do! You take this toxic water, literally death-dealing poison, and you turn it into safe, healthy, life-giving water. I'm wondering: Are you a member of a church, a part of a worshiping community? And do they know what you do—that you literally take waters of death and turn them into waters of life? What a blessing you provide! Do they recognize this ministry you do? Do they celebrate it and honor you for it and pray for you in doing it?" The technician looked at the teacher with quiet surprise.

He was a regular member in a congregation, but it had never occurred to him that his work was a ministry that others might want to affirm and to celebrate as God's work. Such an honoring, though, or even commissioning, I am suggesting, would be a relevant theological response informed by a contextualized analysis of water in that locale. It would be much more appropriate, moreover, than a message about water conservation—even if that message were generally true and genuinely offered but not contextually informed.

Reflections in Water: The Ocean

As I think further about water in other contexts in which I have served, I am aware that the particular contexts of water have occasioned analyses that in turn have prompted theological insights. I served in the Pacific islands at the Pacific Theological College in Fiji, which had a faculty and a student body from throughout the islands of Polynesia, Melanesia, and Micronesia. In that context, I became aware that there are tens of thousands of islands throughout Oceania—an area covering approximately a third of the planet's surface. Yet, there are remarkable cultural similarities throughout the region; the indigenous people as far apart as Hawaii and New Zealand, for instance, can understand much of each other's languages. The symbol of the Methodist Church in Fiji and Rotuma is an outrigger canoe with a cross on its sail—a variation of the boat widely used to symbolize the church ecumenically and historically. The church spread by sea and by sea travelers, by boat.

Growing up on a continent, I had always thought of islands as being separated by water. Once immersed in the Pacific, however, I came to see islands as connected by water. Water is the highway between islands. It is the means through which people travel and the means by which the gospel travels. A familiarity with the ways in which water has historically connected the peoples of the Pacific has consequently expanded my theological understanding of what it means to be a gathered church, a connectional church, and a missional church. Though gathered in congregations, we are connected historically and continually—even with sisters and brothers beyond the horizon. Moreover, there is no place so isolated that it is beyond the reach of God's saving grace. I have become more aware of biblical references to islands and coastlands, such as Psalm 97:1, which exclaims, "The

LORD reigns; let the earth rejoice; / Let the many islands be glad."[12] My neighbors in the Pacific would interpret to me this reference to islands as a declaration of God's sovereign love toward them in particular, as an indication of God's regard for them from the very beginning (from even before the arrival of Christian missionaries), as a connection between them with God's activity throughout the world, and as inspiration for their own missionary activity carrying this proclamation of God's sovereignty to others. Water is not a barrier but a bond between the peoples populating the Pacific, connecting them with each other, with the entire ecumenical church, and with the rest of the world.

Reflections in Water: The Reef

There is great worry throughout the Pacific concerning global warming contributing to rising sea levels which, in turn, would make many of the lower-lying islands uninhabitable. A key factor in an island's habitability is the presence of potable water. Habitable coral atolls maintain a lens of fresh, potable water. Rising sea levels threaten this supply of fresh water with salinization. The primary cause of this problem is the increase of greenhouse gases, such as carbon dioxide, generated primarily in the industrialized and industrializing areas of the world. Internationally, the nations of Oceania tend to be very supportive of multilateral measures to reduce greenhouse gas emissions.

Locally, though, the inhabitants of low-lying atolls are not without some power. Atolls are protected by a fringing reef alive with coral. Corals grow slowly, but a healthy reef will grow faster than an unhealthy one. Reefs are key to the production of sand, forming the atoll itself, and key to the protection of that atoll's freshwater lens. Reefs can be damaged, however, by overexploitation (such as the harvesting of coral rock) and by pollution (such as the release of sewage or fertilizers). Corals are actually the result of a symbiosis between the invertebrate coral animals themselves and particular algae called zooxanthellae, which thrive in nutrient-poor water. When the waters surrounding a reef become overfertilized, other algae outcompete with the zooxanthellae to the coral's destruction. A community of people living on an atoll can give their island the best chance of survival by maintaining a lifestyle consistent with sound reef ecology. At the Pacific Theological College while I was there, the curriculum attended both to the

12. *New American Standard Bible.*

A Constructive Approach

importance of advocacy in international forums for regulation of industrial activity and to the importance of local practices of stewardship for people living literally on the balance between water and land.

This contextualized analysis of reef ecology has theological implications. This became apparent to me in Fiji unexpectedly with regard to the subject of Sabbath observance. Most indigenous Fijians take very seriously the observance of Sabbath on Sunday. Sunday is called *Siga tabu*, or "holy day." It is a time for church and for fellowship. It is not a time for work or commerce. People dress in their Sunday finest for church. In recent years, there was even a coup d'etat in the Fijian Methodist Church over the issue of national laws pertaining to the Sabbath.[13] To visitors from places that were historically a part of Christendom, this all looks anachronistically familiar. One might be reminded of nineteenth-century customs about Sabbath observance in Europe or America, which are more relaxed now. I thought I knew about Sabbath observance in Fiji because of my familiarity with Sabbath observance in my own culture and because of the apparent similarity between the two.

One Sunday, I was walking on the reef at low tide. I stooped down occasionally to catch small tropical fish caught in tidal pockets in order to look at them more closely and to appreciate their beauty. A Fijian man observing from an adjacent bluff called out to me and respectfully asked me to stop "collecting." In fact, while very courteous, he was quite insistent. "It is Sunday," he explained, "the reef needs to rest." I was surprised by his explanation. I thought I knew about Sunday. I realized at that moment, though, that the Fijian *Siga tabu* has as much to do with a particularly Fijian understanding of *tabu* and the Fijians' own history of life on the land within these reefs as it did with any Western traditions or even with the biblical roots of Sabbath observance. The observable familiarity of the form of Sabbath observance to my eyes had actually obscured the subtle but profound difference in its meaning across cultural contexts.

Given the problem of rising sea levels, however, an understanding of reef ecology gives heightened prominence to this Fijian understanding of Sabbath and of community—that the living and worshiping community on Sunday and on any day includes the reef, that the reef along with the human recipients of God's mercy is given the Sabbath, that Sabbath is for both human rest and reef recovery.

---

13. Heinz, "Sabbath in Fiji as Guerrilla Theatre."

These examples pertaining to water illustrate the importance of deepening exploration of contextualized experience in order to inform theology. Water is pervasive in human experience. The particularities of water in a given context, however, provide a bridge to further analysis, whether of polluted aquifers transformed into potable water, islands connected by canoes and historical patterns of migration, or rising sea levels and the ecology of reefs. In each instance, the particularities of a local situation guide the direction of further exploration and analysis. This exploration and analysis then opens theological reflection to new, contextualized insight. In these examples, this process led to new, contextualized insight about theology of vocation, ecclesiology, and Sabbath respectively.

Options for the church's practice and ministry might flow from these insights. Some of these have already been mentioned. In the first example about the aquifer, the teacher suggested that the technician's congregation could celebrate his life-giving work as vocation. Indeed, such celebratory acknowledgment of the laity's vocation in the world could be ritualized in much the same way that the church celebrates the vocation of those being ordained to ministry of Word and Sacrament.

In the second example about ocean passage between islands, we began to consider the implications for an ecclesiological understanding of ecumenical and historical connection. This might have implications for the ways we engage in mission and the ways that we might hold ourselves accountable to a broader understanding of church. In fact, the Pacific Theological College developed a program for mission training and exchange of mission personnel called "God's Pacific People,"[14] with the starting premise being this very understanding of connection between the islands.

The third example, concerning Sabbath rest for the reef, as we noted, has practical implications both locally and globally—for the practice of sound reef ecology by communities inhabiting fragile atolls and for the practice of advocating for international measures to curb the emission of greenhouse gasses. In each instance, we have traveled around the pastoral cycle: from (1) solidarity with people in an actual community to (2) an analysis of the social significance of water in that community to (3) theological reflection informed by that analysis to (4) implications for ministry drawn from that well of theological reflection.

---

14. Pacific Theological College, "God's Pacific People," http://ptc.ac.fj/?page_id=338/.

A Constructive Approach

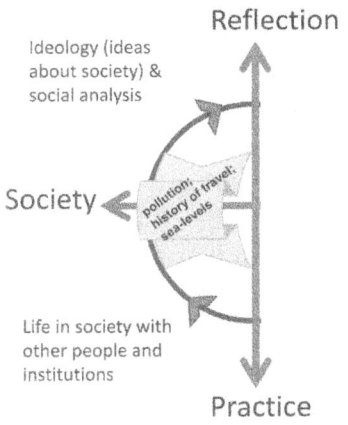

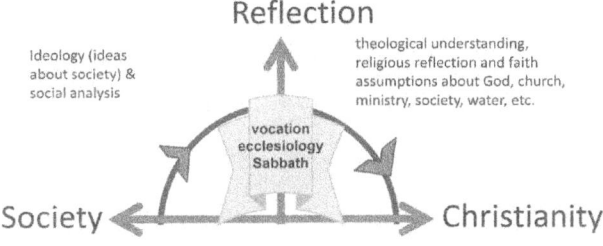

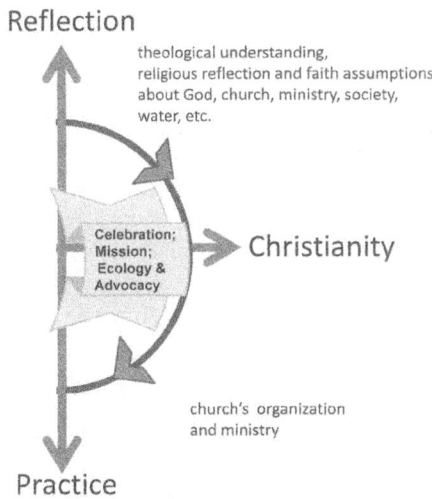

121

Exercise

Perhaps you used the four quadrants of the matrix reflexively at the end of the previous chapter in order to analyze your own theological statement or your own practice of ministry. If so, return to that grid now, and look for the bridge notions (or the bridge practices) between the quadrants in your earlier diagram. What connects the ideas or the practices listed in each quadrant with the ideas or the practices in the adjacent quadrants? As you think about it now, what new ideas or practices occur to you that might have the potential for making this kind of bridge? Write them down in the areas bridging the relevant quadrants. If you have time, perhaps you could now even compose a constructive essay further developing these connections or making them more explicit.

A Constructive Approach

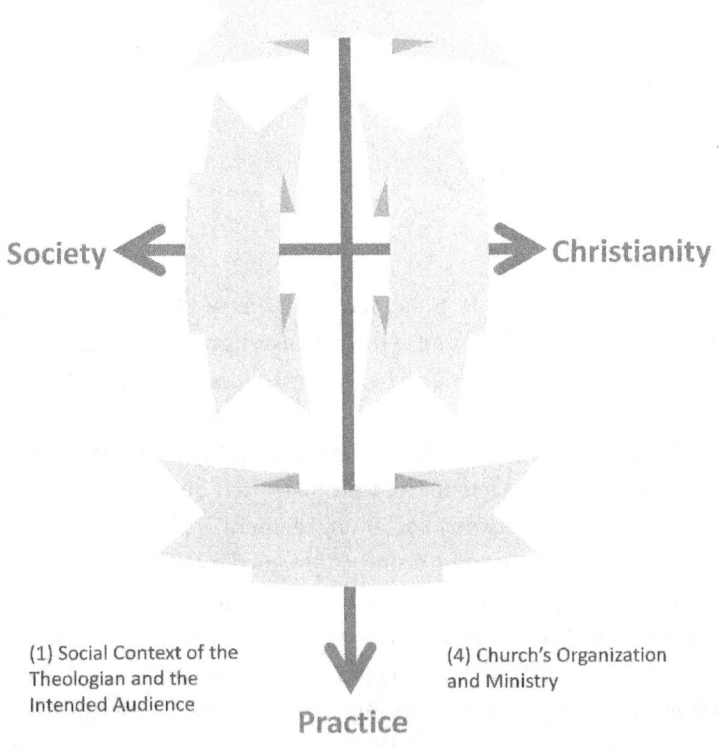

8

Liberation Theology

IN THE EXAMPLES IN the last chapter, we traversed the pastoral cycle in a clockwise direction, beginning with (1) insertion and solidarity within a local community, and moving to (2) contextualized social analysis, then to (3) socially informed theological reflection, and finally to (4) theologically inspired implications for the church's practice of ministry. We noticed that Joe Holland and Peter Henriot had proposed ten questions that presented one way of bridging between social engagement within a community and social analysis within that community. Informed by social analysis, Holland and Henriot then proceed to theological reflection and pastoral planning. Their version of the Pastoral Circle names each of the four movements through the quadrants as (1) insertion, (2) social analysis, (3) theological reflection, and (4) pastoral planning.[1] The Pastoral Circle thus looks like this, beginning with insertion in a community and moving around in a clockwise direction:

---

1. Holland and Henriot, *Social Analysis*, 7–8; "Pastoral Circle" and "Center of Concern" are trademarks of Center of Concern (www.coc.org).

Liberation Theology

Clockwise is not the only way to traverse this methodological circle, however. It is possible as well to travel counterclockwise.

During the years I was in seminary preparing for pastoral ministry, I was very much concerned about the problem of world hunger, and I was able to be active in ministries where I could engage this concern with others. I preached in congregations for the Baltimore Conference Hunger Task Force, raising the problem of hunger in the context of worship. I was involved in three food cooperatives. I served as a research assistant for concerned individuals at the World Bank who were interested in religious values and economic development. I was involved in Bread for the World, a citizens' movement organized interdenominationally among churches in order to advocate among lawmakers concerning hunger.[2] Through all this involvement, I was able to study the problem of hunger from various political, economic, and sociological frames. My personal sense of solidarity with those suffering from hunger motivated my study, and my studying about hunger informed my ministry and my preaching. I was convinced of the need for a political solution to hunger as a political problem. I remain so concerned and so convinced. Looking back, though, I realize now that I was moving through this pastoral cycle in clockwise fashion, much as we have so far been discussing.

In my first parish after graduating from seminary, I was appointed to serve as pastor in a community very much like the Costello parish described above. It was a postindustrial city marked by poverty and hunger.

2. Bread for the World, http://www.bread.org/what-we-do/.

PART 2: METHODOLOGICAL MOVEMENTS

The charitable distribution of food to the community was already an important service that the congregation was providing even before I arrived. Having been committed to political advocacy as a means of addressing the problem of hunger more systemically, though, I asked my ecclesial superior appointing me to this ministry if this congregation had moved beyond service to advocacy in their work on hunger. "Were they involved in politics?" I asked.

"Oh no," my district superintendent replied, "I think that would divide this church right now." So I was advised by my ecclesial superior to avoid politics at least initially as I lived and worked with this congregation, and I followed his advice—at least initially. I stayed involved myself at a political level. I remained involved in Bread for the World, and my wife and I served as congressional district coordinators for that organization. But I confess, I did not try hard to involve my congregants in this aspect of ministry. I encouraged them to continue in their service to the hungry in that community by distributing food, but I shied away from encouraging a more political stance, thinking (patronizingly thinking, I now realize) that political action might prove disruptive to their community and to their ministry.

One morning I woke up suddenly hearing talking and banging. Looking out my window to the church yard next to the parsonage, I saw several parishioners—mothers and their children—who were making signs and nailing them to boards. "What're you all doing?" I hollered down to the yard.

"We're making signs," they said. "There's an adult bookstore opening just over here on Main Street, and we want to stop them. You want a sign, Joe?" I came down. They gave me a sign. We walked down the block to Main Street and started picketing. After a while, the mayor arrived and made a speech in public support of our demonstration and its goals. The adult bookstore did not open.

It occurred to me that my district superintendent had been wrong—and that I was wrong—in assuming that my congregants would not be inclined toward political action. They were the ones who put the placard in my hands. Why, contrary to my assumptions and expectations, were they so very willing and able to effectively engage a political action of this kind? One piece of the puzzle might be the polis itself—the political context. The political context was their own immediate neighborhood; it was not the nation's capital or the state's capital. They were not to be disenfranchised within their own community and concerning the welfare of one another's children. Second, the action emerged directly from their fellowship as an aspect of the ministry of the congregation. It was as immediate an expression of Christian love as their sharing of food with their neighbors.

Looking back, I realize now that they were moving through the pastoral cycle in a counterclockwise direction. Still beginning with solidarity within a particular community in a social context (lower left quadrant), they engaged in ministry directly in response to the challenges presented in that social context. They did so whether it was a matter of feeding the hungry locally or of preventing the influence of pornography among the children of their neighborhood. They moved directly from social solidarity to the church's praxis in that society. The cycle here looks like this:

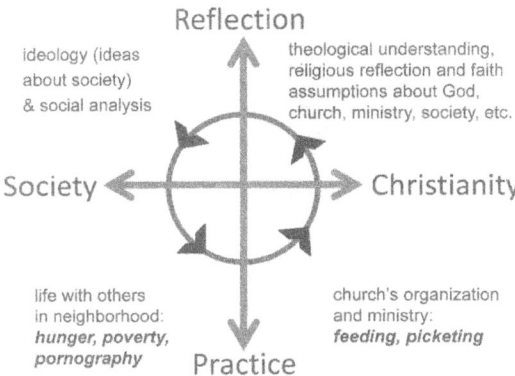

The next move, then, was for us to reflect together on the meaning of our action, to notice what we were doing as a response to God's call to serve in this community in much the same way as feeding the hungry was a call to "do onto the least of these" among us. Further reflection on political action as faithful ministry might move them to consider whether their theological commitments are consistent with or resistant to other ideologies and values in the larger society. This, in turn, might motivate them to expand their political witness into other venues and contexts for action or advocacy, such as the legislatures of the state or nation. The cyclical movement of action-reflection between church and society can proceed in either direction—either clockwise (from context to social analysis to theological reflection) or counterclockwise (from context to ministerial response to theological reflection).

The Argentine liberation theologian José Míguez Bonino makes a very similar point in his book *Toward a Christian Political Ethics*. He too

PART 2: METHODOLOGICAL MOVEMENTS

begins with social solidarity in a particular community, which he calls simply "political praxis." Beginning with such political praxis in solidarity with people as they struggle for justice, he asks how we might articulate a theology of such social engagement. He argues that there are two "mediations" by which Christians might arrive at such a socially and contextually engaged "theology of politics." One mediation is clockwise through "social theory," represented here in the upper-left quadrant. The other mediation is counterclockwise through the political praxis of Christians represented here in the lower-right quadrant. Using Míguez Bonino's language, our circle would look like this:[3]

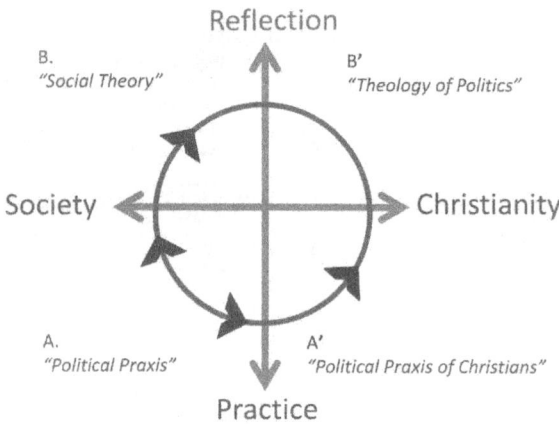

Referring to each of these quadrants as A, A', B and B', José Míguez Bonino explains:

> There are two fruitful approaches. These can be described in terms of connections signified in the diagram. The A → A' → B' connection suggests that Christian reflection on political praxis can be mediated by the experience of Christians engaged in political action. Here A' constitutes a first and indispensible hermeneutical key, the discernment of Christian faith and love, which acts out its obedience by assuming a historical praxis that is then subject to critical reflection on the basis of Scripture and Christian tradition.
>
> The A → B → B' connection suggests that Christian reflection on political praxis can be mediated by secular social theology. Here B represents an equally necessary scientific key, the theoretical elaboration of a political praxis that is again assumed and then

3. Míguez Bonino, *Toward a Christian Political Ethics*, 48.

subjected to critical reflection from the standpoint of specifically Christian faith.[4]

The second of Míguez Bonino's possible mediations—that of making use of social theory—was my initial predisposition in the story that I relate above. For me, coming out of an academic environment into a new community context and into my first role as pastor, I found that theory helped me make sense of the social situation in order to better articulate my faith and my faith commitments in that situation. My presumption had been to move from the concrete situation to social theory and then to theology. This had served me well (and it still does). I discovered that my congregants had a disposition in the other direction—the first rather than the second of Míguez Bonino's proposed mediations—from the social situation to a directly engaged response as Christians and then to reflect further on their praxis as Christians. This had served them well (and I imagine still does). Beginning from the concrete situation, both directions are possible. Both are potentially productive and constructive as Christians minister together and reflect together about their shared praxis in society.

Exercise for Reflection:

For this exercise, please contemplate an actual social context and/or an actual situation of ministry in which you are currently engaged with others. As you look at the four quadrants of our chart, how do you find yourself navigating through them? Do you tend to move clockwise or counterclockwise around the circle? In which quadrant do you begin? Where do you end up? Is your movement stymied at any point along the way?

Now please turn your attention to your fellow collaborators in this ministry or to your neighbors in this social context. How do they navigate between these quadrants? Do they tend to move clockwise or counterclockwise? Do some move in one direction and others in the other direction, or do they all tend to move in concert together? Where do they begin? Where do they end up? Is the cyclical process of action-reflection in church and society continuous, or does it get frustrated at some point?

Now compare your own preferred style of negotiating these quadrants with that of your congregants, collaborators, or neighbors. How are you alike or different in this regard? How might you yourself make better use

---

4. Ibid, 49.

of the ways they proceed around the circle—their presumed methodology? How might you together more fully navigate these quadrants to further resource ministry in your community or to further inform your theological understanding of ministry in that community?

Moving either A → A' → B' or A → B → B' (to use Míguez Bonino's shorthand), how do you start to sketch out B' more fully? That is, how do you start to articulate a Christian theology of politics? Or, more generally, how do you further articulate your theological understanding about God, church, ministry, society, and so forth as a result of having moved through these quadrants?

As we become increasingly familiar with this cyclical method, it becomes apparent that it is actually a rather natural way of engaging in practical theology. We naturally find links between our theological thinking and our practice as Christians, between our practice as Christians and our shared social realities in community, between our understanding of these social realities and our theological affirmations as people of faith. We make these connections whether explicitly and intentionally in scholarly fashion or more tacitly and intuitively simply as Christians engaged in faithful living. We all do this, in other words. Practical theology really is "practical." This simplicity, or even elegance, of the cyclical method of practical theology should be appreciated before we move further.

We need to appreciate the simplicity of this method, because it sometimes appears quite complex as we listen to the different voices of theologians utilizing it. Each theologian provides their own nuance to this methodology, and they use their own language for naming the movements through the circle. The remainder of this chapter and the next will attend to some of these theological voices and notice the language they employ for navigating the cyclical method. In the process of providing this comparison between these theologians, much of their respective nuance will be backgrounded in order to highlight the methodological commonality between them. Readers are urged to refer to the writings of these theologians themselves in order to discover the reflective richness of each. The aim here, though, is to display the methodological similarity.

So far we have introduced both the Pastoral Circle of Joe Holland and Peter Henriot and the similar method of José Míguez Bonino. Since these theologians are working with a framework shaped by liberation theology, it might be helpful at this point to compare their methodological language with that of the influential liberation theologian Juan Luis Segundo. Segundo articulated his "hermeneutic circle" in the mid-1970s. Beginning with our experience of social reality (especially of social injustice and oppression), Segundo moves to "ideological suspicion" of society's justification of injustice. This leads him to "hermeneutical suspicion" of the ways that Christian theological interpretation may have been distorted by the influence of the dominant ideology. This hermeneutical suspicion of Christian theology then leads to the development of a "new hermeneutic" for interpreting the Christian faith. Segundo explains:

> *Firstly* there is our way of experiencing reality, which leads us to ideological suspicion. *Secondly* there is the application of our ideological suspicion to the whole ideological superstructure in general and to theology in particular. *Thirdly* there comes a new way of experiencing theological reality that leads us to exegetical suspicion, that is, to the suspicion that the prevailing interpretation of the Bible has not taken important pieces of data into account. *Fourthly* we have our new hermeneutic, that is, our new way of interpreting the fountainhead of our faith (i.e., Scripture) with the new elements at our disposal.[5]

This new hermeneutic has "experiential" implications for the ways Christians both articulate and live out their faith in church and society.[6] Placed together on our schema, these theological methods move through the same pattern—uniting practice with reflection and uniting Christian response to social realities and ideologies.

---

5. Segundo, *Liberation of Theology*, 9.

6. Ibid., 232; both Segundo and Míguez Bonino acknowledge the influence on their thinking of a school of thought from Germany in the early twentieth century pertaining to Christian social ethics and to sociology of religion. Segundo (ibid., 19–25) cites Max Weber's *Protestant Ethic and the Spirit of Capitalism* in demonstration of the methodological bridge from ideological suspicion to Christian hermeneutical suspicion. Míguez Bonino cites Ernst Troeltsch exemplifying the need to "relate praxis (both secular and Christian) and theory (both socioanalytical and theological)" (*Towards a Christian Political Ethics*, 37–38, citing Troeltsch, *Social Teaching of the Christian Churches*, 1:30–33). For a discussion of the relation between Weber and Troeltsch, see Bush, *Gentle Shepherding*, 141–42, 198. My appreciation of the importance of Troeltsch for both liberation theology and practical theology as well as for Christian social ethics has been influenced by Thomas Ogletree, *World Calling*, 11–41.

Part 2: Methodological Movements

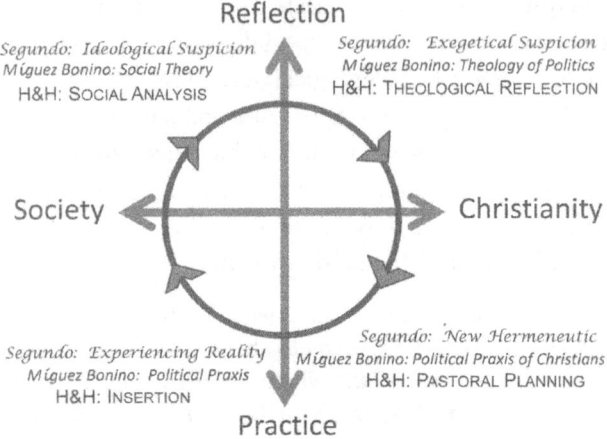

The pastoral cycle was similarly developed in the context of the United Kingdom by Laurie Green. Green credits both Juan Luis Segundo and Paulo Freire as inspiration for his development of the pastoral cycle, and he notes its similarity with that developed by Holland and Henriot in the United States.[7] Green's iteration of the pastoral cycle is quite elegant with regard to the commonsense designations he uses to name each of the moments. He uses succinct verbs to emphasize the active aspect of doing theology.[8] Starting from "experience," he names the subsequent movements sequentially as: "explore," "reflect" and "respond." He cites Segundo with approval that "'Any and every theological question begins with the human situation.'"[9] Explicit theological reflection then follows out of the experience and analysis of this human situation. We will return to Green later to see how his approach to explicit theological reflection can be particularly helpful as we reflect on experiences in ministry.

Green draws his pastoral cycle in a different direction than we have so far been using, but if we place his methodological moments within our schema alongside those of Segundo, Míguez Bonino, and Holland and Henriot, our schema now looks like this:

---

7. Green, *Let's Do Theology: Resources*, 18.
8. Laurie Green, personal correspondence, 18 May 2012.
9. Green, "Why Do Theological Reflection?" 18n3.

Exercise for Reflection

Please return to the social context or situation of ministry that was the subject of your attention in the previous exercise for reflection earlier in this chapter. Recall the differences you might have been noticing between your own approach to this situation and that of your fellow collaborators in ministry or of your neighbors in the social context. Does the language of any of the theologians schematized above seem more accessible than others? If you were to engage collegially with your neighbors in further analysis of the social situation or in further theological reflection about it, what language among these options might best facilitate your conversation together? What language might help you to move ahead together most productively? If you are reading this book in concert with others, discuss this together. What seem to be the advantages or disadvantages of the ways these movements are named in the four quadrants? What particularities of emphasis or nuance might be important to you?

In this chapter, we have compared four different iterations of a liberationist method that connects experience with reflection and that does so in a way that also links Christianity with the wider social/political/economic/cultural world. These four methods have been compared: Segundo's hermeneutic circle, Holland and Henriot's Pastoral Circle, Green's pastoral cycle, and Míguez Bonino's "mediations." We noticed in particular with

Míguez Bonino that the movement of this method through our quadrants can actually—"in practice"—happen in either direction. Most of those who articulate this kind of method, though, tend to follow the pattern of moving (1) from experience in society to (2) a deepening understanding of social realities to (3) explicitly Christian reflection to (4) the practice of Christian ministry. This is the clockwise direction in our schema, at least in the way we have been drawing it.

As a method for liberation theology, this approach was developed by Latin American theologians such as Segundo and Míguez Bonino in the 1970s. It soon found expression in the English-speaking world as well; Holland and Henriot provide an example of this in the North American context, and Laurie Green provides an example in the context of the United Kingdom. In the 1980s another theological movement with similar methodology took shape. This is the renewed interest in "practical theology" to which we turn in the next chapter.

9

Practical Theology

THE PHRASE "PRACTICAL THEOLOGY" has a very long history in theological study. It constituted one of the three main divisions of theology in Friedrich Schleiermacher's *Brief Outline on the Study of Theology* in 1811 and 1830, these three being: philosophical theology, historical theology, and practical theology.[1] Renewed attention to practical theology as a discipline, though, occurred in the 1980s. In America, the Association of Practical Theology was formed in 1984. Shortly after the end of the decade, in 1991, the International Academy of Practical Theology was formed.[2] Two short anthologies on practical theology were published during this decade and proved very influential. *Practical Theology: The Emerging Field in Theology, Church, and World,* edited by Don. S. Browning, appeared in 1983, and *Formation and Reflection: The Promise of Practical Theology,* edited by Lewis S. Mudge and James N. Poling, appeared in 1987.[3] These were multidisciplinary volumes whose contributors were well-respected scholars in the fields of pastoral care, systematic theology, social ethics, biblical studies, and Christian education. Much of the energy for this renewed interest in practical theology was devoted to the effort of attending theologically beyond more narrow foci on the particular arts of Christian ministry.

Writing in practical theology, these scholars were interested in forging a greater methodological integration of theological reflection with

1. Schleiermacher, *Brief Outline on the Study of Theology.*
2. International Academy of Practical Theology, "History." http://www.ia-pt.org/history/.
3. Browning, *Practical Theology*; Mudge and Poling, *Formation and Reflection.*

PART 2: METHODOLOGICAL MOVEMENTS

practices broadly conceived. The current statement of the Association of Practical Theology explains:

> The purpose of the Association of Practical Theology (APT) is to promote critical discourse that integrates theological reflection and practice. Reconstituted from its predecessor organizations 1984, the APT was sparked by the investigation of practical theology as an integrative hermeneutical endeavor at the heart of theological education, characterizing not only the ministerial subdisciplines but also a manner and method of engaged reflection.[4]

This interest in the method of practical theology inspired renewed efforts to articulate the relationships between theory and practice, between theology and other disciplines of thought, and between the church's praxis and the wider social context. Not surprisingly, these renewed methodological efforts often took cyclical forms that have distinct parallels with the methods we have already been discussing.

This chapter will attempt to chart some of these methodological iterations on our grid, much as was done with liberationist methods in the previous chapter. The point of this exercise is to elucidate some of the commonality between them. Deeper comparisons can be made only by attending to each thinker's own statements about their method and by relating them to the statements of others. Actually, a brief comparison delineating the commonality between two of the most influential of these practical theologians—Don Browning and Thomas Groome—has already been offered by Robert Schreiter in the handbook, *Studying Congregations*.[5] Before we look at Schreiter's comparison of Browning and Groome, though, we will begin by attending to Edward Farley's description of his method for practical theology. Edward Farley was a contributor to both of the anthologies mentioned above[6] and has been a very influential voice in theological education generally.

Farley emphasizes the importance for practical theology to enable us to interpret "situations." He defines situations broadly: "A situation is the way various items, powers, and events in the environment gather together so as to require responses from participants."[7] His definition is inclusive of

---

4. Association of Practical Theology, "About APT." http://practicaltheology.org/about/.

5. Schreiter, "Theology in the Congregation."

6. Farley, "Theology and Practice Outside the Clerical Paradigm"; Farley, "Interpreting Situations."

7. Farley, "Interpreting Situations," 12.

a broad range of situations. Situations, he clarifies, can be brief or enduring, and they can be local or global. They can be situations of individuals, groups, communities, collectives, or whole societies. Farley's first step is to describe the situation. In his second and third steps, he then moves to interpretation of that situation's past and of the wider situational context. Such interpretation will broaden our understanding of the situation both historically and contemporaneously with other situations. Fourth, explicitly theological interpretation becomes central, and this leads finally to "discerning the situation's demand."[8] Placed on our conceptual grid and cyclical schema along with Holland and Henriot's four movements in parentheses,[9] Farley's method would appear as follows:

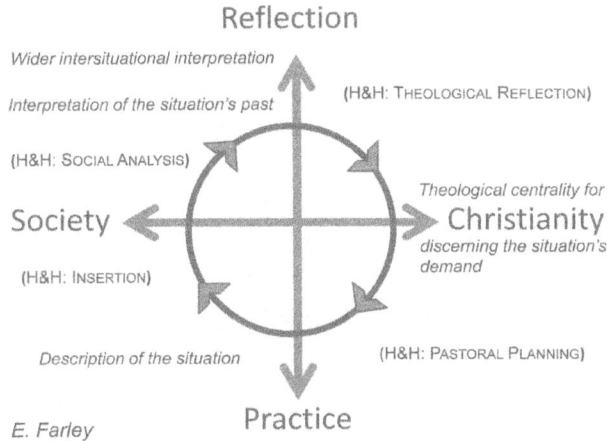

It should be apparent that the breadth of Farley's understanding of "situations," is very similar to the breadth of our understanding of "practice" with which this book began and that we have been assuming throughout these pages. Moreover, Farley's historical deepening and "intersituational" broadening of interpretation is very similar to the way that Holland and Henriot advocate social analysis to expand our understanding of a particular social context. Moving now to the methodologies of Thomas Groome and Don Browning, both Groome and Browning can be seen to show similarities both with Farley's method and with the liberationist hermeneutic

---

8. Ibid., 14.

9. Holland and Henriot, *Social Analysis*, 7–8; "Pastoral Circle" and "Center of Concern" are trademarks of Center of Concern (www.coc.org).

described in the previous chapter. Both Groome and Browning are integrative and profound thinkers who are able to encompass disparate schools of thought even as they distill from many scholarly influences a praxeological method that is accessible in its simplicity. Among these influences on their respective methods are some of the liberationists discussed above. Browning begins his *Fundamental Practical Theology* with such an acknowledgement, naming Juan Luis Segundo and José Míguez Bonino among others,[10] and he indicates, "Segundo's conception of the hermeneutic circle, as stated in *The Liberation of Theology,* is very close to mine."[11] Groome writes of Paulo Freire that he is "the most significant exponent of a praxis approach to education today," and he acknowledges drawing significantly from Freire in developing his own method.[12]

In *Studying Congregations,* Robert Schreiter compares Thomas Groome's "shared praxis" approach to Christian education and ministry[13] with Don Browning's method in *A Fundamental Practical Theology*.[14] According to Schreiter, both Groome's and Browning's methods begin with experience itself and with description of the situation being experienced. "Groome calls this 'naming the present praxis,' and Browning calls it 'descriptive theology.'"[15] Schreiter emphasizes the importance of this initial descriptive moment in practical theology. He summarizes the overall movement of practical theology as follows:

> Practical theology is tied closely to the lives of congregations and individuals. Rather than moving from faith to life (theory to practice), it moves from life to faith and then back to life (practice to theory to practice). Practical theology begins, therefore, by describing the situation of the congregation and then correlates that situation with the faith and the beliefs of the congregation. From there, practical theology moves back to the life of the congregation to a refocused practice.[16]

---

10. Browning, *Fundamental Practical Theology,* ix.
11. Ibid., 66.
12. Groome, *Christian Religious Education,* 175–6.
13. Schreiter cites Groome's *Sharing Faith,* which further develops a method built upon Groome's earlier *Christian Religious Education.*
14. Browning, *Fundamental Practical Theology.*
15. Schreiter, "Theology in the Congregation," 26.
16. Ibid., 25.

Further, Schreiter insists, "describing the situation is part of theological reflection itself, not just a prelude to it."[17]

For Groome, though, this attentiveness to the "present praxis" seems to occur in two movements. There is an initial naming or expressing of one's own or of society's "present action." This naming is the beginning of conscious engagement with that action, practice or situation. But this engagement deepens more critically with Groome's second moment, called "critical reflection on present action," which involves "any or all activities of critical and social reasoning, analytical and social remembering, creative and social imagining." This second of Groome's movements aims at the development of "critical consciousness of the present praxis," which includes "its reasons, interests, assumptions, prejudices, and ideologies (reason); its sociohistorical and biographical sources (memory); its intended, likely and preferred consequences (imagination)."[18] The direction of thought in Groome's first two movements is from experience itself to naming that experience to critically reflecting on that experience. This entails critical reflection on the whole social context shaping the current practice and not attending merely to so-called private experience.

In comparison, Browning's more succinct phrase for his first move, "descriptive theology," also already includes critical analysis and not merely description. This analysis, according to Browning, involves attentiveness to the social sciences in order to display the meanings embedded in practices. At the same time, he distinguishes this hermeneutical approach from the more "narrowly empirical natural sciences."[19] Browning explains the difference: "Social-systemic, material, and psychological determinants are traced and explained as well as possible, but they are placed within the larger set of meanings that give them direction in the scheme of human action. These larger meanings that constitute the theory embedded in our practices invariably have a religious dimension."[20] The focus for Browning in descriptive theology is the uncovering of meaning held contextually in situations. It has already moved beyond the plane of the practice itself to the level of critical reflection on it.

The next movements for both Groome and Browning give explicit attention to the theological resources of communities of faith. Browning

17. Ibid., 26.
18. Groome, *Sharing Faith*, 146–47.
19. Browning, *Fundamental Practical Theology*, 47.
20. Ibid., 48.

names the next movement "historical theology," by which he means a critical attentiveness to the interpretation of normative texts and to the history of theological interpretation. Groome attends very similarly, but he names this movement "making accessible the Christian story and vision." For both Groome and Browning, this movement involves hermeneutics of normative texts in order to display theological meanings emerging out of our religious tradition.

For both Groome and Browning, this then leads to a movement of dialogue between (a) the meanings available to us from our theological tradition and (b) the meanings appearing to us from analyzing our current practices. Schreiter explains: "Practical theology differs from much traditional theological work in the [next] move it makes. Rather than simply using historical sources as a measuring rod against which to critique the current situation, practical theology calls for a conversation between the two."[21] Groome refers to this as a "Dialectical Hermeneutic to Appropriate Christian Story/Vision to Participants' Stories and Visions." Browning refers to this simply as "systematic theology," but Browning clearly is intending such a dialogical process.

This then leads to the final movement for each. Groome refers to this last movement as "Decision/Response for Lived Christian Faith." Browning refers to this simply as "strategic practical theology." In each instance, the dialogical process of reflection between the theological tradition and the analysis of the lived situation now informs the decisions, actions, and practices of the Christian community. Reflection informs Christian practice. Groome's and Browning's movements can be placed on our methodological grid along with Farley's as follows:

---

21. Schreiter, "Theology in the Congregation," 26.

Practical Theology

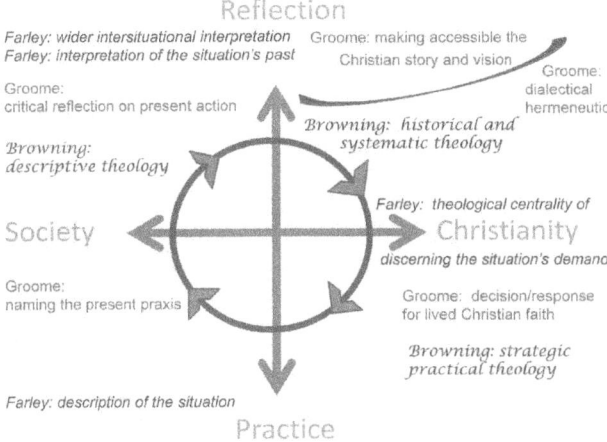

Practical theologians continue to refine this cyclical method of reflecting on practice. In 2008 Richard Osmer published his *Practical Theology: An Introduction*, which has become influential across the field. His language for navigating this method seems succinct and intuitive. He speaks of four tasks of practical theology, beginning with asking simply, "What is going on?" He refers to this initial step as the Descriptive-Empirical Task. An Interpretive Task then follows, asking "Why is this going on?" He refers to the third movement as Normative Task asking, "What ought to be going on?" Finally, we come full circle, responding in practice having been informed by our reflection. He refers to this last as the Pragmatic Task that asks "How might we respond?"[22] Placed on our grid, Osmer's method might look as follows:

---

22. Osmer, *Practical Theology*, 4.

Part 2: Methodological Movements

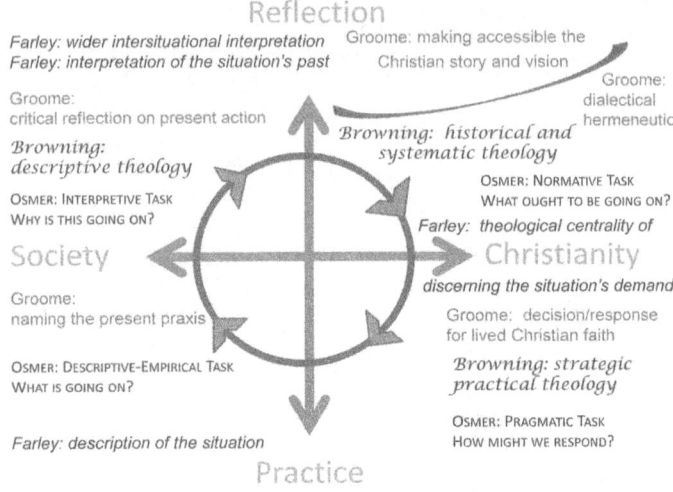

Each of these methods begins with the concrete experience of situations in practice, further describes and interprets these situational realities, brings this broadened interpretation of the situation into dialogue with the deeper theological tradition, and then concludes by articulating the kind of informed and faithful response that might be lived out in practice.

A key moment in each of these methods is the movement between the upper-left and the upper-right quadrants of our grid. The conversation between interpretation of the situation and explicitly theological interpretation occurs as a kind of dialogue. We noticed that Groome refers to this conversation as a "dialectical hermeneutic" between the two. Browning advocates a similar hermeneutical process when he discusses systematic theology. Referring to the hermeneutics of Hans-Georg Gadamer, Browning writes, "Systematic theology, when seen from the perspective of Gadamer's hermeneutics, is the fusion of horizons between the vision implicit in contemporary practices and the vision implied in the practices of the normative Christian texts. This fusion between the present and the past is much different from a simple application of the past to the present."[23] Browning sees this "fusion" or conversation between the tradition and the

---

23. Browning, *Fundamental Practical Theology*, 51, citing Gadamer, *Truth and Method*.

contemporary situation to be a task of systematic theology as a "submovement within a larger practical framework."[24]

Moreover, Browning, Groome,[25] and Osmer[26] all make reference to David Tracy's critical correlational method in making such a move between the contemporary situation and the texts of the Christian tradition. Critical correlation theory seeks to articulate theology by critically correlating between the sources of Christian texts and common human experience and language. David Tracy expanded upon Paul Tillich's earlier method of correlation in developing this method. Tracy advocates a critical correlation between hermeneutical analysis of texts (Christian faith in its many expressions) and phenomenological analysis of common human experience in its cultural expressions.[27] Don Browning, in particular, advocates this approach.

Another way of moving from reflection on the social situation to explicitly theological reflection is suggested by Bishop Laurie Green, whose iteration of the pastoral cycle or theological spiral was described in the previous chapter. The social context for Green and his work are the urban areas of the United Kingdom. Green notices that the experience of ministry in an urban context always seems to entail discoveries and surprises that provoke new insights and intuitions. A new insight or intuition can then help one make connections between exploration of the social context and theological reflection. He articulates a process of theological reflection that takes advantage of such intuition as a kind of ancillary circle within the overarching pastoral cycle. During the phase of reflecting, an intuition arises that leads to further exploration. Green says succinctly that we "check out" the intuition, and this leads to a "new witness." The process allows the intuitive insight to guide our renewed attentiveness to theological resources as we check out the intuition on the way to articulating a "new witness."[28] Placed on our interpretive grid, Green's ancillary circle for reflection might look as follows:

---

24. Ibid.
25. Groome, *Sharing Faith*, 191, citing Tracy, *Blessed Rage for Order*, 64.
26. Osmer, *Practical Theology*, 164–67.
27. Tracy, *Blessed Rage for Order*, 43–45.
28. Green, *Let's Do Theology: Resources*, 96–105; Green, *Let's Do Theology: A Pastoral Cycle*, 90–98; Green, "Why Do Theological Reflection?" 11–18.

Part 2: Methodological Movements

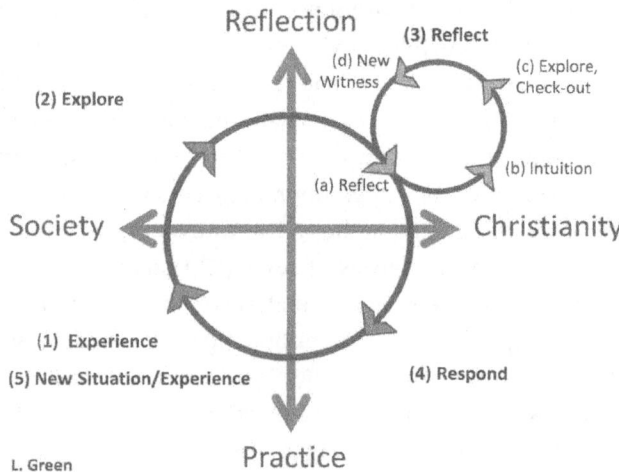

Each of the methodological processes described in this chapter provides a possible bridge between the upper-left and upper-right quadrants of our grid, that is, between our reflective exploration of contextual realities on the left and explicitly theological reflection on the right: critical correlation, Groome's dialectical hermeneutic, or Green's process of checking out intuitions.

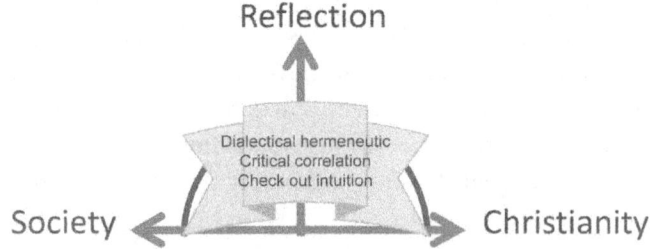

Exercise for Reflection

Chapter 7 concluded with a bridging exercise as follows:

> Perhaps you used the four quadrants of the matrix reflexively at the end of the previous chapter in order to analyze your own theological statement or your own practice of ministry. If so, return to that grid now, and look for the bridge notions (or the bridge practices) between the quadrants in your earlier diagram. What connects

the ideas or the practices listed in each quadrant with the ideas or the practices in the adjacent quadrants? As you think about it now, what new ideas or practices occur to you that might have the potential for making this kind of bridge? Write them down in the areas bridging the relevant quadrants. If you have time, perhaps you could now even compose a constructive essay further developing these connections or making them more explicit.

Return now to that exercise and in particular to the bridge between the upper-left and the upper-right quadrants. Do any of the methods suggested here help you to further bridge between exploration/reflection of the social context on the left and explicitly theological reflection on the right? As you think about this situation and your analysis of it, have you been surprised by either your experience itself or by your reflective exploration of it? Does this surprise or discovery in your social context provoke any insight or intuition of a theological nature? Note: an insight or intuition might not be experienced as epiphany; it might rather be experienced as a quandary or a puzzle or a question. Pursuing that quandary, though, might lead to an epiphany. Try using Laurie Green's method of checking out intuition to further reflect theologically on this same exercise.

10

Solidarity and Suspicion

Practical Theology and Liberation Theology

THIS BOOK HAS INTRODUCED several related approaches to theological method employed by those writing in the area of practical theology. Several of these utilize a version of critical correlation theory. David Tracy actually defines practical theology in terms of this mutually critical correlation: "Practical Theology is the mutually critical correlation of the interpreted theory and praxis of the Christian fact and the interpreted theory and practice of the contemporary situation."[1] In his *A Fundamental Practical Theology*, Don Browning cites Tracy's definition with approval—which he considers to be an "excellent definition" of the "central theological enterprise" that is inclusive of the disciplines of descriptive, historical, systematic, and strategic practical theology.[2]

Critical correlation, however, has not gone without correlative criticism by some proponents of practical theology. An earlier iteration of Don Browning's correlational approach as well as David Tracy's approach to practical theology were criticized by James Fowler, who suggested that—while neither theologian intended to subordinate praxis to theory—they, Fowler nonetheless suspected, had inadvertently substituted an "idea of

---

1. Tracy, "Foundations of Practical Theology," 76, quoted by Swinton and Mowat, *Practical Theology and Qualitative Research*, 79.

2. Browning, *Fundamental Practical Theology*, 47, citing Tracy, "Foundations of Practical Theology," 76.

praxis" for praxis itself. This was encouraged, according to Fowler, by their reliance on hermeneutics, which stresses the problem of meaning and interpretation[3] rather than practical engagement with others in society or in social struggle.

Drawing from liberationist, feminist, and German political theologies, Rebecca Chopp offers a similar criticism of practical theology's limitations. Like Fowler, she argues that the critical correlation method of "liberal-revisionist" theology tends to assume the basic problem to be one of meaning making rather than that of historical engagement within society in need of transformation. Citing liberation theologian Gustavo Gutierrez, she states: "While liberal-revisionist theologians respond to the theoretical challenge of the nonbelievers among the small minority of the world's population who control the wealth and resources in history, liberation theologians respond to the practical challenge of the large majority of global residents who control neither their victimization nor their survival."[4] The very "point of religion" for liberation theology, according to Chopp, "has to do with emancipation and enlightenment of persons in history,"[5] as opposed to determining the veracity of cognitive faith claims of the more privileged people within the increasingly secularized part of the world. Since liberation theology is not primarily concerned with the "crisis of cognitive claims," according to Chopp, it does not really need a "theoretical method of correlation." She cites Matthew Lamb in this regard:

> As Matthew Lamb has demonstrated, the nature of the correlation in the liberal-revisionist approach is always a theoretical correlation. The limits of this theoretical correlation lie in the dominance, and even the hegemony, of theory over praxis.[6]

In contrast, liberation theology "needs a method that can critique and transform situations."[7] The two methods, she suggests, are in tension to the point of being incommensurable.

Praxis is understood differently in each of these methods, Chopp argues. While praxis is typically understood by liberal theologians as intentional activity, Chopp contrasts, liberation theologians tend to understand

---

3. Fowler, "Practical Theology and Theological Education," 55.

4. Chopp, "Practical Theology and Liberation," 128, citing Gutierrez, *Power of the Poor in History*, 212–13.

5. Chopp, "Practical Theology and Liberation," 129.

6. Ibid., 131, citing Lamb, *Solidarity with Victims*, 75–76.

7. Ibid.

praxis "in a broader sense of the web of social interactions."[8] The purpose of praxis in liberation theology, according to Chopp, is to "transform and 're-make' history"[9] and not simply to correlate normative views with existing practices, thus privileging "balancing or reconciling meanings."[10] The political intent of praxis is unavoidable for liberation theologians, who believe that "all theology is political," as opposed to viewing politics as just "one distinct arena of praxis," as Chopp contends is typical of liberal-revisionist theology.[11]

Since Fowler's criticism in 1985, both Tracy and Browning have deepened and nuanced their writing about theological method to take into account this criticism and to give greater emphasis to the importance of social praxis. Browning has taken account of liberationist criticisms of correlational method, in particular of Matthew Lamb and of Rebecca Chopp.[12] Tracy's *Analogical Imagination*, which was not cited in Fowler's article, had actually already been published; it provides a stronger emphasis on praxis and identifies particular realms or publics to which theology might be oriented, e.g. practical theology as being oriented toward the social public.[13] Nevertheless, Fowler's and Chopp's insightful criticisms stand as reminders that practical theology should not be too vastly abstracted from the world of practice and action—of society and culture as well as church.[14]

Indeed, this issue concerning the nature of praxis and of "practices" continues to be ingredient in current developments in practical theology. Written more recently, Richard Osmer's *Practical Theology*, published in 2008, makes due note of Rebecca Chopp's and Matthew Lamb's liberationist critique. In particular, Osmer acknowledges the critique that "the real crisis confronting theology is not one of meaning but one of human suffering," and he indicates the goal of theology's dialogue with other fields should be to "contribute to social transformation that alleviates this suffering."[15] He

8. Ibid., 133.

9. Ibid., 132.

10. Ibid., 135.

11. Ibid.

12. Browning, *Fundamental Practical Theology*, 47, citing Chopp, "Practical Theology and Liberation," 120–38, also citing Lamb, *Solidarity with Victims*.

13. Tracy, *Analogical Imagination*, discussed by Lamb, *Solidarity with Victims*, 80.

14. For further discussion of this debate, see Hastings, *Practical Theology and the One Body of Christ*, 4–12.

15. Osmer, *Practical Theology*, 167, citing Lamb, *Solidarity with Victims*, ch. 3, also citing Chopp, "Practical Theology and Liberation," 120–38.

defines a "revised praxis method of correlation" as follows: "the first and most important dialogue is between movements and communities sharing common emancipatory goals. The dialogue between theology and other fields is a second step, arising out of transforming praxis and helping to guide this praxis."[16] Tellingly though, even with this emphasis on the primacy of transformative social praxis, Osmer discusses this matter in his chapter pertaining to the "normative task" of practical theology rather than in the descriptive-empirical task. This would still seem to place the concern at the level of making meaning rather than at the level of concrete social engagement as the necessary beginning for emancipatory theology.

Also published in 2008, *For Life Abundant: Practical Theology, Theological Education, and Christian Ministry* was funded by the Lilly Endowment and has contributions from many highly respected voices in practical theology, including the volume's editors, Dorothy C. Bass and Craig Dykstra. Dorothy Bass defines "practice" for that volume as follows:

> This summary of a theological and normative understanding of practices interprets practices as the traditioned yet always-emerging patterns through which communities live as Jesus' disciples, responding to God's grace and to the needs of human beings and all creation. It interprets practices, in short, as forms within and through which a Christian way of life takes shape.[17]

In a footnote, Bass responds to Laurie F. Maffley-Kipp, Leigh E. Schmidt, and Mark Valeri, whose book, *Practicing Protestants* (also sponsored by the Lilly Endowment), contrasts her understanding of practices as benevolent with a social-scientific perspective that "adopts a critical stance toward the power arrangements embodied in practices."[18] Bass acknowledges that her understanding of practices does tend to assume "each Christian practice as a whole as good" even while, she contends, incorporating "critical and self-critical perspectives."[19]

---

16. Osmer, *Practical Theology*, 167.

17. Bass and Dykstra, *For Life Abundant*, 32.

18. Maffley-Kipp et al., *Practicing Protestants*, 1–6; on pp. 3–4 the authors are quoting Bass's earlier definition of "practices" as "those shared activities that address fundamental human needs and that, woven together, form a way of life. Reflecting on practices as they have been shaped in the context of Christian faith leads us to encounter the possibility of a faithful way of life, one that is both attuned to present-day needs and taught by ancient wisdom" (Bass, *Practicing Our Faith*, xi).

19. Bass and Dykstra, *For Life Abundant*, 30n10.

It does seem that two different ideas of practice are at play in this conversation—or at least two very differently nuanced understandings of practice. One is looking at "Christian" practice in particular—though this might be a wide range of different kinds of Christian practices engaged in by both individuals and organizations. The other is looking at "practice" as that broader "web of social interactions," to use Rebecca Chopp's phrase, and the power entailed in those relations. Moreover, there seem to be two different interpretive stances from which to view these two different ideas about practices. There is a relatively trusting view that practices—explicitly Christian practices—are benevolent and formative for Christian community. This is contrasted with the more suspicious view that practices—even church practices—are complicit with inimical forces at work within the wider web of social relations.

For Christian practical theology, this book has argued, we need to consider both our distinctively Christian practices and the broader social realities encompassing Christian organization and activity. The logic of our method helps us to focus attention on both kinds of practices and their relationship to each other. We have tended to demark our participation in specifically Christian practice within the lower-right quadrant of our interpretive grid, and we have attended to the relationship between these Christian practices and the wider society on the left side of that interpretive grid. The cyclical method moves our attention between the quadrants, so that we continually ask about the influential relationship between the two—between our practices as Christians and our practice within a wider society. How does one give shape to the other? How does one constrain the other? This method allows us to distinguish between them in order to better evaluate their continuing connection with each other in real life, that is, in practice. We are enabled to see and to critique Christian practice within its wider social context.

The liberationist critique, however, reminds us that the social forces at work in society are not simply the context environing Christian practice; they are the forces shaping Christian practice. Correlatively at the level of reflection on practice, social ideologies give shape to Christian theologies. From this perspective, we have seen argued, priority must be given to immersion and solidarity with those in society who are striving for justice. Otherwise, the church can find its theology and practice simply reflecting if not justifying prevailing social conditions. From this perspective, right thinking and just acting begin in social solidarity, which provides a condition for the continuing reform and correction of Christian theology and practice.

It can be seen that all of the cyclical methods described in this book allow us to navigate between Christian practice, social realities, social analysis, and theological reflection. The liberationist models, however, emphasize the importance of engagement with and attention to "practice" pertaining to the very social realities shaping (or distorting) human existence. (This was represented on the lower-left quadrant on the methodological grid.) The other practical theological methods that we have compared allow—and even encourage—this movement as well, but the necessity of engaging the wider social dimension as a matter of both praxeological and epistemological priority is not always as salient as it is in the avowedly liberationist methods. It is certainly the case that all of these methods for practical theology have been informed by liberation theology and its methods. Liberation theology's priorities, however, such as the epistemological privilege of the poor, are not always as pressingly apparent in their methodological unfolding.

There may still be some merit in the contention of Fowler and Chopp that it is the very reliance of practical theology on hermeneutics that tends to focus attention primarily on issues of meaning and interpretation rather than as urgently on the practice of engagement with others in their struggle for justice.[20] It is the case that liberation theologians emphasize the necessity of concrete engagement in social praxis. However, hermeneutics is also at the core of liberation theology, as we have seen from our own methodological journey in chapter 8 of this book with the hermeneutical circle drawn by Juan Luis Segundo. For liberationists, hermeneutics is grounded in social struggle and is employed in the service of projects for social transformation. Segundo's hermeneutical circle begins with the experience of social reality and moves to ideological suspicion and to hermeneutical suspicion. It would seem that the particular role of suspicion in hermeneutics that characterizes the liberationist approach may be key in this debate.

Paul Ricoeur

Paul Ricoeur's distinction between a hermeneutics of suspicion and a hermeneutics of restoration might guide us at this point. Ricoeur distinguishes between a hermeneutics of suspicion that aims at uncovering

20. Fowler, "Practical Theology and Theological Education," 55.

hidden, disguised, or encrypted meanings in a text and a hermeneutics of restoration that aims at recollecting, or displaying the meaning of a text as intended and understood by the author(s) of that text. Both types of hermeneutics assume that one is challenged to understand or interpret the meanings inherent in another's text or another's communication. The main difference between them pertains to whether one is primarily attentive to the author's/speaker's understanding of that meaning or if one is critically suspicious of the author's/speaker's perspective and finds meaning through a critical process of reinterpretation. The meaning ascertained through a hermeneutics of suspicion might be hidden to the original author or speaker, and the interpreter's explication of that meaning might seem quite foreign to him or her. For examples of a hermeneutics of suspicion, Ricoeur points to the writings of Freud, Marx, and Nietzsche.[21]

Ricoeur maintains this distinction between approaches to hermeneutics not only with reference to texts as documents but to other fields of inquiry marking his work, including "the theory of texts, the theory of action, the theory of history, and psychoanalysis."[22] At its most basic, Ricoeur refers to this hermeneutical distinction as attending differentially to both comprehension and explanation. While comprehension requires a sympathetic reading in order to better understand, deeper explanation follows from critical lines of inquiry that approach the subject with greater suspicion. While this distinction in hermeneutics has been described as a "conflict of interpretations," Ricoeur explains that this is not a conflict "*between* interpretations" but "*within* interpretation." Both approaches are needed. Ricoeur insists, "My contention is that understanding without explanation is blind as much as explanation without understanding is empty."[23]

Throughout this book on practical theology in church and society, both a hermeneutics of restoration and a hermeneutics of suspicion have been employed at various points in our discussion. In chapters 3 and 4, a hermeneutics of restoration can be seen to be operative in use of the ladder of inference in Farber-Robertson's method of case study and in use of the "practical hermeneutics grid." Each of these exercises is designed to help the interpreter attend more carefully to the meaning that the other individual might be intending to convey or be bringing to the situation. These exercises do so, however, by means of different strategies. The use of

---

21. Ricoeur, *Freud and Philosophy*, 28, 32
22. Ricoeur, "Conflict of Interpretations," 223.
23. Ibid., 225–26 (italics original).

the ladder of inference in case study helps the interpreter step aside from his or her own inferential interpretation in order to attend more deliberately to the actual data in the discourse. Such inferential interpretation, we saw, could be laden with suspicion about the other's motives that might actually hinder communication because of projection and blame. The "practical hermeneutics grid" employs a different strategy but toward the same end. Instead of moving down the ladder of inference to attend more deliberately to actually spoken words, it asks us to brainstorm about the many possible interpretations of a phrase that we might infer in a pastoral encounter. But this process then asks us to choose the "most generous response" from among these many possible interpretations. In each case, the exercise is designed to help us attend more closely to the meanings that might be intended by the other by holding our own suspicions or inference in abeyance.

Both a hermeneutics of restoration and a hermeneutics of suspicion are present in chapter 1 with regard to social location, in chapter 2 with regard to "stereo vision" when encountering congregational culture, and in chapter 3 with regard to liminal leadership. In each of these chapters, the dynamic between insider and outsider is highlighted. The pastor is seen as both insider and outsider at once within a congregation's culture and its surrounding community. This presents a challenge to the pastor to be able to attend more deliberately to intended meanings of parishioners in their communications together. At the same time, the role of suspicion comes into play in recognizing the influence of social location in shaping a person's priorities, commitments, and interpretations. Because of the liminal status of the pastor as both insider and outsider, the pastor is able to bring both an emic (insider's) and an etic (outsider's) interpretation to situations within the parish.

A hermeneutics of suspicion has been employed in the chapters pertaining to liberation theology and in the comparisons of various cyclical reflective methods with the hermeneutic circle of Juan Luis Segundo. As we have seen, Segundo's method gives prominent emphasis to the role of suspicion in critiquing both ideology and biblical/theological hermeneutics. Segundo was influenced by the thought of Karl Marx pertaining to class struggle and class consciousness. The key idea here is that prevailing social ideology reflects and reinforces economic privilege, and further that a critical consciousness is conditioned upon engagement in class struggle alongside the underclass in efforts to reorder society. Marx's critical perspective about the determining influence of economic class on ideology influences liberation theology in giving import to solidarity in class struggle as the necessary context for engaging in theological reflection.

However, drawing on Ricoeur's hermeneutical distinction, we might find that solidarity with those struggling for justice actually demands a sympathetic listening toward respectful comprehension as much as it does a suspicious attention leading toward deeper explanation. Ruthellen Josselson, a psychologist interested in the narrative interpretation of people's lives, draws on Ricoeur's distinction between these two interpretive stances in reaching such a conclusion. She writes:

> Ricoeur demonstrates that the hermeneutic interpretive stance, in its derivation from philosophy and interpretation of sacred texts, can be positioned in two different ways. The first positioning aims at the *restoration* of a meaning addressed to the interpreter in the form of a message. It is characterized by a willingness to listen, to absorb as much as possible the message in its given form and it respects the symbol, understood as a cultural mechanism for our apprehension of reality, as a place of revelation. This type of hermeneutics is animated by faith. By contrast, hermeneutics may be approached as the demystification of meaning presented to the interpreter in the form of a disguise. This type of hermeneutics is characterized by a distrust of the symbol as a dissimulation of the real and is animated by suspicion, by a skepticism towards the given. Ricoeur suggests that it is the latter type of hermeneutics which is practiced by Marx, Nietzsche and Freud. All three of these 'masters of suspicion' look upon the contents of consciousness as in some sense 'false'; all three aim to transcend this falsity through a reductive interpretation and critique.[24]

Even though Marx, mentioned here as a "master of suspicion," is widely understood to champion the cause of the oppressed in social conflict between economic classes, Josselson prefers a hermeneutics of faith or restoration over a hermeneutics of suspicion when seeking to hear and to understand the voice of the marginalized and oppressed in society. She continues:

> As researchers, our effort is to unearth the meanings inherent in the narratives we obtain, remaining faithful to the (multiple and layered) intentions of the narrator, rather than trying to construct them differently. This approach is of paramount value when our

---

24. Josselson, "Hermeneutics of Faith and the Hermeneutics of Suspicion," 3.

aim is giving 'voice' to marginalized or oppressed groups and thus representing their experience.[25]

The aim, according to Josselson, is to give credence to the understanding of the marginalized themselves as they are able to find expression. One wants to avoid their further disenfranchisement by overlaying on top of theirs another layer of meaning inferred by the interpreter according to the interpreter's preconceived theory. Although interpretation always is the construct of the interpreter, the aim here is for the interpreter to understand as closely as possible the meaning that might be held by the speaker.

Conclusion

In this chapter we have noticed the continuing relevance of a critique of practical theology that has been voiced from a liberationist perspective. While this critique was levied primarily at the use of critical correlation theory within practical theology, it challenged more broadly the assumptions about "practices" and indicted the very priority given to meaning making in hermeneutics. In response, we have noticed with appreciation ways practical theologians such as Don Browning and Richard Osmer have addressed these concerns, and we have attended to the hermeneutics of Paul Ricoeur for help in addressing this critique ourselves. We found Ricoeur's distinction between a hermeneutics of suspicion and a hermeneutics of restoration helpful for articulating ways in which both hermeneutical stances might be present in practical theology. Indeed, we have suggested along with Ricoeur that both might be necessary.

This chapter has also tacitly touched on some other questions related to the role of hermeneutics in practical theology. These questions pertain to the relationship of ourselves as interpreters with other actors and agents in any given situation. Is our activity as practical theologians outwardly focused on the world of practices and practical reality, or is it inwardly focused on ourselves either as actors or as interpreters? Is practical theology a corporate activity that is conducted cooperatively and publicly with others, or is it more privately accomplished by individual interpreters? What is the role of reflexivity in our practical theology? How is our practical theology about us, and how is it about others? This book actually began with these questions as we distinguished between individual actions and wider areas

---

25. Ibid., 6, citing Tappan, "Analyzing Stories of Moral Experience."

of practice. We began by affirming the importance of reflecting on ourselves and on our own actions as individuals within a given social location. To these questions of reflexivity this book now returns in the concluding chapter.

Exercise for Reflection

Throughout this book there have been "exercises for reflection," in which a tool for reflection on practice has been introduced, or in which readers have been asked to reflect on practice utilizing the interpretive grid or the cyclical method. Look back over your reflections in these exercises. This chapter has highlighted two interpretive stances—a hermeneutics of restoration in which we attempt to listen as closely as possible to others' intended meanings, and a hermeneutics of suspicion in which we bring a critical eye to bear in attempting to enrich our explanation of events and practices. While a hermeneutics of suspicion may be especially prominent in a liberationist approach, this chapter has affirmed the presence and necessity of both hermeneutic approaches in our reflection on the practice of ministry in church and society. As you look over your own reflections in the exercises of previous chapters, where do you see yourself employing a hermeneutics of restoration? Where do you see yourself employing a hermeneutics of suspicion?

11

Reflexivity

Looking Back, Looking Ahead

THE PREVIOUS CHAPTER EXAMINED some concerns about practical theology, especially as voiced from a liberationist perspective. These concerns raised questions about the idea of practice. In particular, whose practice is of concern in practical theology? By "practice," do we mean the actions of individuals, the practices of the Christian community, or the larger web of social relations and historical forces? We affirmed that we need to attend to practice at each of these levels, and we recognized that the cyclical method explicated in this book allows us to do so. In fact, this method at its best posits the question of the relationship of Christian practices to social praxis from the outset. As we have seen, the very name "practical theology" describes a dialogue between theological reflection and the so-called practical. That is, it is a praxeological method, which is reflection on practice. Such practice is broadly conceived to include not only individual actions of ministry in church and society but also those larger social and cultural forces which act on us—that shape our ideas and that both constrain and potentiate our individual actions and our churches' ministries.

A further, related question pertaining to practice was also raised in the previous chapter. This is the question of whether or not practices are considered benign and even beneficial—helping to develop a people of virtue, helping us to deepen in Christian discipleship and faithful living. Or, conversely, when understood as that web of social relations and social forces, is social practice inimical to the greater good, distorting of Christian witness, requiring from us a practical commitment to engage in struggles for social justice? This question drew us to a consideration of the role of suspicion in hermeneutics and, in particular, to Ricoeur's distinction between a hermeneutics of suspicion and a hermeneutics of restoration. Again, we affirmed the need for both approaches in our interpretation of practice.

Now, in this final chapter, we attend again to the importance of individual agency in self-reflection, recognizing that as individuals we are thoroughly enculturated and shaped by social and cultural influences. Throughout this book, we have described practical theology as reflection on practice, and we have recognized that *practice* can refer to multiple levels of individual action, organizational processes, and larger social realities. For people of faith, theology is important at each of these levels, whether individual beliefs and commitments, ecclesial affirmations and confessions, or efforts to discern God's ongoing activity in the whole inhabited world. We have engaged in reflection focused both outwardly on our social community and inwardly on our own participation as individuals in church and society. When our reflection is self-reflection focused reflexively back on ourselves, we refer to this as reflexivity. This book began with such reflexive attention to ourselves acting as individuals with social location. This final chapter now returns to the matter of self-reflection with an appreciation for the complexity of social and cultural forces that shape us.

As we have seen, some social and cultural influences work to our benefit and virtue, others to our detriment and to the distortion of both our self-understanding and our life together. Much has already been said in this book about the influence of the larger social world—economic and political forces as well as cultural influences—on both our practice and our reflection, whether as individuals or as church. We are right to attend with suspicion to these social forces even while we trust both in God's grace and in the redemptive possibilities for life in society. The significance of the wider culture for practical theology, I believe, is dual—influencing both reflection and practice. Culture is constitutive of that world of ideas that shapes our thinking and, correlatively, it is constitutive of that social "practice" that informs our Christian practice.

When we think about culture and about ourselves as enculturated, we notice a mutuality of influence. Each is formed by the other. We can speak of the cultural construction of the self, realizing that at a most fundamental level we as persons are the products of our culture. But culture is itself the product of our human construction, the product of our life together as multiple individuals over time. The first half of this final chapter attends to this matter of mutual relationship between ourselves as individual persons and ourselves together as constituting culture. In particular, we will focus on the idea of reflexivity or self-reflection in understanding this relationship. The chapter will then conclude with some thoughts about pedagogy and formation in light of the kind of reflectivity being advocated here.

Cultural Theory and Self-Reflection

It may initially seem as if we are presented here with two different foci for our attention—either inwardly in self-reflection or outwardly toward the social and cultural world. While this tension does denote different directions demanding our attention, it does not represent a mutually exclusive choice. As we have already recognized, reflective individuals and their cultures are mutually formed.

Cultural theorist Clifford Geertz makes the case for the constancy of culture in shaping humanity by pointing out that humanity's culture and biology have coevolved. According to fossil evidence, Geertz argues, our primate ancestors at their earliest were already social animals creating meaning in interaction with one another and establishing patterns in those interactions. Geertz defines culture in terms of semiotics, emphasizing the importance of symbolism as constituting a shared system of meeting. A shared symbolic system allows us to interact meaningfully with one another. He writes:

> Undirected by cultural patterns—organized systems of significant symbols—man's [sic] behavior would be virtually ungovernable, a mere chaos of pointless acts and exploding emotions, his experience virtually shapeless. Culture, the accumulated totality of such patterns, is not just an ornament of human existence but . . . an essential condition for it.[1]

He further explains:

> When seen as a set of symbolic devices for controlling behavior, extrasomatic sources of information, culture provides the link between what men [sic] are intrinsically capable of becoming and what they actually, one by one, in fact become.[2]

---

1. Geertz, *Interpretation of Cultures*, 46.
2. Ibid., 52.

Culture is not just a set of symbol systems that are themselves the constructs of human subjects; it is a set of symbol systems and practices that help shape our very humanity and our meaning-making capacity.

As we have seen, many writers in practical theology attend to culture as a methodological moment in theological construction. This emphasis on culture in constructive theology has provided a grounding of theology in the social realities and the thought-worlds of particular peoples—an "outward" focus on the social and cultural community. This intent can be seen, for instance, in Robert Schreiter's 1985 book *Constructing Local Theologies,* in which he suggests that all theology is local theology.[3] At the same time, however, a reflexive turn in cultural studies has reminded students of culture about the importance of their own reflective processes, of a more "inward" focus, even as they attempt to construct an account of the cultures they are discovering. Both the inward focus on self and the outward focus on culture are important for the way we have been approaching the task of practical theology in this book.

As theology attends to culture, though, we face two methodological difficulties. First, one difficulty has to do with the normative task of theology taking into account cultural content or cultural critique. How does one make the shift from description and analysis of cultural patterns of human interaction and human meaning toward the more explicitly normative construction of theological positions? Chapter 9 suggested certain movements of thought or strategies to help us bridge between specifically Christian theological reflection and the wider world of ideas within our culture or about our culture. These movements helped us bridge between the upper-left and upper-right quadrants of our methodological grid. Critical correlation theory is one of these strategies. Similar to critical correlation method, Laurie Green's ancillary cycle aims to deepen "insight" that moves between the exploration of cultural context and the articulation of theological construction. Green's cycle, we saw, is largely dependent on insight and intuition. These methods do not posit specific theological norms. Rather they facilitate dialogue between ideas pertaining to a particular culture and to the Christian tradition. The Christian tradition holds myriad affirmations, confessions, and interpretations that can function normatively in this dialogue. This first problem or difficulty with the role of culture in practical theology, though, has to do with theology's normative task taking

---

3. Schreiter, *Constructing Local Theologies.*

into account the formative if not normative importance of culture in shaping Christian thought and practice.

Even if culture is not considered to be a source of norms for theological reflection, however, it nonetheless constitutes that symbolic system from which all reflection arises. It is a de facto source for theology even if it is not affirmed as a normative one, since culture encompasses our entire world of thought. Thus, the second difficulty we face as practical theologians attending to cultural realities is related to culture itself as a shaper of ideas. In addition to the first question of theology's normative task as it attends to Christian texts and tradition in cultural context, practical theology faces a parallel challenge as it attends to culture itself as an arena of meaning making. The challenge we face as practical theologians in this regard has its corollary with other disciplines of study and with cultural theory itself.

We face a dilemma—or at least a tension—in contemporary cultural theory pertaining to the way culture and personal agency are perceived in their relationship to each other. The tension resides in the question of mutual influence—or even of determination—between our cultures, which provide the symbol systems that make all reflection possible, and ourselves as individual reflective persons. Do we emphasize the relative power of culture to shape our very humanity and ourselves as reflective individuals, or do we emphasize our power as humans in constructing our own cultural reality? On one hand, culture is acknowledged as a powerful shaper of social practices, ideas, and values. On the other hand, however, a reflexive turn in cultural theory focuses attention back to the agency of the individual as a reflective subject.

Kathryn Tanner describes this tension well. She notes that the power of culture in shaping human life and action is one of the "basic elements" of an understanding of culture that was developed by anthropologists during the twentieth century. Tanner writes: "Because culture is constitutive of humanity and cultures are aligned with social groups, *the notion of culture suggests social determinism: society decisively shapes the character of its members.*"[4] Referring to cultural "norms for action" Tanner, however, further explains:

> Norms for action may be part of culture. . . [but] in assuming such norms are responsible for social order commits, moreover, the fallacy of normative determinism: because norms are meant

---

4. Tanner, *Theories of Culture*, 28 (italics original).

> to control behavior, it does not follow that they actually or successfully do so . . .
>
> In criticizing the modern understanding of culture as a social-ordering principle one need not deny that the beliefs, values, and so forth of a culture influence the sort of action that participants find appropriate; affirming such an influence is part of the postmodern proposal of a politics of culture. . . What is wrong with the modern idea of culture as an action-governing principle is the suggestion that culture has certain social effects on its own apart from the specific uses made of it by historical agents.[5]

Human agency is thus reaffirmed even while we find ourselves ensconced in culture. How then are we to understand this agency?

If we are to answer this question about our agency as enculturated individuals while taking into account the liberationist critique of "practices" and the discussion about a hermeneutics of suspicion from the previous chapter, we might consider the following. At the very least, we would want to become better able to know ourselves and to name and recognize the social and cultural influences shaping our own thought-world, even while we are encountering—especially while we are encountering—other people and other cultures. To take the influence of culture on individual thought and action seriously, it would seem, actually heightens the importance of our reflective attention to ourselves as individual actors and thinkers with social location.

In the area of cultural studies, a landmark work along these lines has been Talal Asad's *Anthropology and the Colonial Encounter*.[6] Published in 1973, this anthology shows how ethnographers' accounts of cultures throughout the world can reflect the worldviews and the agendas of the colonial centers. The book presents a challenge to ethnographers to be both critical of the historic projects that frame cultural encounters and self-critical of their own complicity with those colonizing perceptions and interests. As a theologian reading it, I find a similar challenge toward deeper self-reflection to be relevant for all of us engaged in practical theology as we attend to culture as the context for theological reflection.

The reflexive turn in cultural studies, however, has been further sharpened by even more radical understandings of reflexivity in critical cultural theory. In its extreme form, some, such as Frederick Steier, have argued that

---

5. Ibid., 49.

6. O'Reilly, *Ethnographic Methods*, 210, citing Asad, *Anthropology and the Colonial Encounter*.

all one does is to reflect back on oneself apart from any objective reality beyond oneself as the thinking subject.[7] However, for practical theologians who are interested in engaging others in reflecting meaningfully on human relationships and shared meanings, such radical epistemological skepticism misses the mark. Ironically, practical theology has attended to culture in order to ground theological reflection praxeologically in the social realities that shape human existence and in the shared structures of meaning within which we live and understand our living. Such a radical reflexive turn as suggested by Steier, though, would seem to constitute a U-turn—returning us to the ivory towers of our own thoughts—albeit thoughts concerning the world and the church's praxis within that world.

Of course, reflexivity is always necessary in any disciplined endeavor to understand ourselves or our world. John Swinton and Harriet Mowat, in their book *Practical Theology and Qualitative Research*[8] present two dimensions of reflexive knowledge that are necessary. Personal reflexivity has us examine our own assumptions and commitments when we engage in scholarly research or reflection. Epistemological reflexivity has us asking questions about our methods of investigation and our knowledge of the objects of our inquiry—questions pertaining to veracity, validity and reliability. Some degree of epistemological reflexivity, it can be argued, must be ingredient in any project of research or reflection. For practical theology, though, I want to affirm that personal reflexivity is particularly important at three levels.

First, to be a reflective practitioner requires such personal reflexivity, and action-reflection models of learning presuppose it. For those preparing for service and leadership in religious organization, action-reflection is particularly designed into programs of personal and professional formation—such as theological field education for seminarians and clinical pastoral education. Action-reflection has the student reflect on him/herself in ministry in order to deepen self-awareness as prerequisite for more deliberate and effective pastoral interactions. Earlier chapters of this book, especially chapters 3 and 4, emphasized this aspect of personal reflexivity and introduced some tools for action-reflection in pastoral ministry.

---

7. Steier, "Research as Self-reflexivity, Self-reflexivity as Social Process," cited by McLeod, *Qualitative Research in Counselling and Psychotherapy*, 195.

8. Swinton and Mowat, *Practical Theology and Qualitative Research*, 60, citing Willig, *Qualitative Research in Psychology*.

Second, personal reflexivity helps us to identify our participation in oppressive realities and to attend to alternative narratives that might promote liberation. This aspect of personal reflexivity is broader than self-awareness alone. It has to do with awareness of oneself as formed in constant relationship to others. At this level of personal reflexivity, we recognize that we are being constrained or empowered by the constellation of social forces within which we live. Sociology of knowledge has reinforced this insight that our perceptions, thoughts, insights, and values all reflect and respond to our social locations. Reflexivity at this level reminds us that we must be cognizant of our social locations and their influence on us. It is for this reason, as we have seen, that Holland and Henriot's Pastoral Circle begins with insertion into a particular community.

Third, and paradoxically, greater personal reflexivity allows us to engage others more authentically. One might expect that reflexivity would tend to focus one's attention solely back onto oneself. However, it seems to be the case that such self-awareness frees one to be more attentive to others at the same time. Becoming aware of one's own thought processes and emotional responsiveness allows one to attend with greater clarity (with less personal clutter) to others. This is a helpful skill both for pastoral theologians providing pastoral care and for leaders of religious communities, who are challenged to understand those communities to which they have been called. Probably all ministry in community is cross-cultural to some degree. Greater reflexivity allows a pastor entering a new congregation or community to be more aware of both his or her own assumptions and the differences that he or she encounters in the lifeways and thought processes of those with whom she or he is in ministry. Self-awareness, in other words, seems to correlate with sensitivity to others.

Reflectivity and Praxeological Education

Throughout this book we have conceptualized the task of practical theology in church and society with reference to two dialectical relationships informing our work: the relationship between reflection and practice, and the relationship between church and society. To reiterate, practice was seen to refer at several levels to the practices of individuals, of organizations, and of the larger society. We affirmed that even the actions of individuals must be seen with reference to wider social communities environing and shaping us as individuals. We acknowledged that an individual's social location was

Reflexivity

always ingredient in that individual's choices, actions, and reflections. One unavoidably does theology from a position provided by social location. We take into account both one's own given location in social praxis as well as one's commitments in solidarity with others in social praxis.

In these last two chapters, this book is now concluding by acknowledging a liberationist critique that further emphasizes the importance of social location for practical theology. From this liberationist perspective informed by sociology of knowledge, social location is thought to be very influential, if not actually determinative, of perception. It would even appear from this liberationist perspective that just thinking and right acting are both premised upon ones identification with those who have been marginalized and oppressed. Epistemologically, we have suggested, a good methodological beginning for theological reflection is insertion within a particular community and solidarity with the people struggling for justice within that community.

Programs in theological field education deploy seminarians in contexts of ministry in order to provide them with an epistemological point of reference for their learning within a particular community. These programs operate with a set of assumptions related to the process of learning in community. Four such assumptions seem particularly relevant as we conclude this book on practical theology in church and society with an eye toward possible implications for ministerial education. First, there is a pedagogical assumption that self-awareness will develop within the context of ministry in collaborative relationship with others. Second, it is assumed that congregations themselves are located within broader social contexts that provide an opportunity for ministry with people beyond the congregation's walls. Third, it is assumed that those placed in ministerial internships can establish meaningful relationships with others that can contribute to their formation for ministry. Fourth, it is assumed, often tacitly, that a sound epistemological beginning in solidarity with others is also an effective pedagogical point of departure—a kind of praxeological prerequisite for further learning. While these are reasonable assumptions, they also can be questioned. They will each be discussed below. Programs in theological field education have the potential to engage students most meaningfully in practical theological reflection, it will be suggested, to the degree that these assumptions hold true.

First, there is the pedagogical assumption that self-awareness will develop within the context of ministry in collaborative relationship with others. Because of this emphasis on learning contextually in community, some of these programs are named "contextual studies" or "contextual education." They are meant to move beyond merely applying lessons learned in a classroom to a field setting.[9] They are meant to provide opportunity for deeper integration beyond the honing of particular skills in the arts of ministry. The context of ministry itself, it is hoped, will be formative for the students as they are involved in meaningful relationship with others. However, as one of my colleagues likes to remind us, "Practice does not always make perfect."[10] Sometimes we simply practice bad habits. Moreover, conversation partners in the reflective process—whether classmates, congregants, or supervisors—can inadvertently reinforce self-justifying rationalizations rather than encourage new insight in their effort to be supportive. Rather than simply assuming that meaningful reflection will occur, reflection on practice needs to be intentionally taught, nurtured and embraced in order for it to foster greater self-awareness and deeper integration of learning. Practice of ministry alone does not necessarily promote new learning, but it can provide a condition for new learning in theological reflection.

Most ministerial internships for theological field education occur in congregations. The second assumption that the wider social context of these congregations provides further opportunity for reflective engagement in social praxis may actually be more of a hope than an assumption, since many congregations do not fully avail themselves of the opportunities for service provided by their locations in community. All are located in some social context nonetheless, and that opportunity for broader social engagement between the congregation and the wider community continually arises.

In order to provide grounding of theological reflection experientially in the lived struggles of people, some programs in theological education endeavor to augment traditional congregation-based field education with opportunities for service learning. That is, they provide students with opportunities for service in neighborhood associations, public policy advocacy groups, community organizations, charitable missions, health care providers, and governmental organizations. As we have seen, it can be

9. My colleague at United Theological Seminary of the Twin Cities, Barbara Anne Keely, would emphasize this distinction saying, "we do not give credit for field work at United but for contextual study." My thanks to Prof. Keely for introducing me to the work of Jody D. Nyquist and Jo Sprague described below.

10. Sondra Ely Wheeler, who is Professor of Christian Ethics at Wesley Theological Seminary, also team-teaches field education colloquies.

argued that solidarity with a particular public must be taken into account from the outset of theological study. For this reason, some programs in theological education seek to provide entering students with experiences in service learning from the very outset. The idea is to begin theological education with social praxis. Such insertion within a community working for justice gives students something of a common ground of experience upon which to build their theological education.

Solidarity, however, is not easy. This brings us to the third assumption that ministerial interns can establish relationships that contribute to their formation for ministry. Relationship-building requires work. Moreover, it requires openness, and many factors might mitigate against such openness to relationship. This is especially the case when the new relationships being established require a bridging between cultural differences or between differences established by our respective social locations. Because of the challenge entailed in building relationships and in establishing solidarity in new cultural contexts, this book has devoted considerable attention to the dynamics between insiders and outsiders. Initially it may seem peculiar to question the third assumption that ministerial interns can establish meaningful relationships with others, since all of us continually establish such relationships. At the same time, though, we realize that we establish boundaries as well, especially when the new relationships being established might challenge our own sense of comfort with ourselves and our self-understanding. Yet such solidarity with others in their struggle for justice and well-being, we have recognized, is considered foundational if we are engaged in practical theology from a liberationist perspective.

Even without such a liberationist orientation, however, building solidarity with others remains a challenge in congregational ministry. Theological students often are introduced to the study of congregations concurrent with their field education internships in ministry. Contemporary study of congregations, we have noticed, has been particularly informed by a cultural understanding of organizations. This perspective emphasizes the human dimension of institutional life and the values—often irrational—that motivate people to participate in institutional life and mission. The idea is that ministerial students who are able to appreciate this cultural, often extrarational, dimension of congregations will be better equipped to work with real-life people in their common purpose—whether this has to do with compassionate pastoral care or with effective leadership for vital congregations and their missional outreach. As with the liberationist approach to practical theology, so too this congregation-centered approach assumes the capacity of the student/intern/minister to enter into solidarity with a particular social community—whether a neighborhood or a congregation. Reflection is understood to proceed from such insertion and solidarity within a community and that community's practice.

This brings us to the fourth assumption concerning the methodological affinity between our epistemology in practical theology and our pedagogy of formation for ministry. That is, it is assumed that the theological method that begins with shared practice in community translates into an effective pedagogical method as well. In fact, an identity between the two—between valid epistemological method and effective pedagogical process—is often assumed.

As we have seen, the epistemological beginning in practice is variously named: "description of the situation" (Farley), "descriptive theology" (Browning), "naming the present praxis" (Groome), "insertion" (Holland and Henriot), "experience" (Green), descriptive-empirical task" (Osmer), "experiencing reality" (Segundo), and "political praxis" (Míguez Bonino). These writers vary in the degree to which they might consider such a beginning in practice to be a necessary point of departure for theological engagement, but they all posit it as at least a beginning point for theological reflection in social context. They also vary to the degree that they emphasize the social dimension of practice in community with others, but that social dimension is nonetheless unavoidably present.

At this point, however, I want to notice an irony. Epistemologically, our methods of practical theology tend to begin with experience and practice in community. However, this valid epistemological or methodological beginning point actually requires a very high level of skill. This is especially so, I believe, for students beginning the process of reflection on practice, not attending simply to individual actions but to practice within the larger social community. It is a well-developed capacity to be able to attend with sensitivity and percipience to a larger world of shared practice and diverse meaning.

While beginning with solidarity in community provides a promising epistemological point of departure, it thus also entails a pedagogical challenge. Such solidarity and social-perspective taking requires a complex set of skills involving cognitive, affective, and kinesthetic capacities. The development of these capacities to engage others authentically and compassionately might even seem to represent the fruition of one's formation for ministry—maybe even the fruition of a lifetime of ministry. This is an irony: the sound beginning point epistemologically can constitute an elusive point of departure formationally, because it requires such a high level of skill to have already been acquired. Pedagogically, we might need to begin to stage the development of such capacity with initial and incremental steps.

What might these steps be? There may be parallels between the developmental process of formation for ministry and developmental processes of formation for other professions. If so, these parallels might provide insight toward identifying incremental steps in professional development for ministers.

Jody D. Nyquist and Jo Sprague and their colleagues conducted a longitudinal study of graduate students as they developed from being teaching assistants (TAs) to becoming professors. Midpoint in their study they noticed that these novice teachers seemed to develop a greater capacity over time to understand and appreciate their students as learners. These researchers posited a process of development of this capacity. Initially, these researchers suggested, teaching assistants often seemed most concerned about their own personal comfort level having to do with both familiarity with the course material and confidence in their own competence for the jobs assigned to them. With more experience, they tended to become more interested in the curriculum itself and in its pedagogical effectiveness. Only with further experience and maturity, the researches suspected, were many better able to focus outwardly on their students themselves as learners. Nyquist and Sprague summarize this development as follows:

> At the earliest stage, concerns center on self and survival. TAs worry about what to wear, how their students will address them, whether they will look and sound enough like an instructor to gain respect, and whether they will please their students and employers. After initial experiences, TAs' concerns tend to center on issues related to mastering the skills of teaching such as lecturing, leading discussion, grading, and constructing exams. Only at a somewhat advanced point, when there is a reasonable comfort level in the instructional role and some degree of proficiency in teaching, do TAs' concerns turn to the impact of instruction. It is then that they worry most about whether their students are learning, and if not, how best to assist them.[11]

---

11. Nyquist and Sprague, "Thinking Developmentally about TAs," 68.

Part 2: Methodological Movements

The initial period is marked by a concern with oneself and the way one is regarded by others—whether by students or by faculty. The intermediate period focuses less personally on self and acceptance and more technically on the effectiveness of the curriculum and the tasks of teaching. The final period, which was not always attained, is marked by a greater possibility of genuine interest in the other—in the way others learn.

As the longitudinal study unfolded, these researchers found they were not able to sustain this developmental pattern in any strict sense, as they encountered too many variables operating and too much individual variation among their subjects.[12] A key variable for promoting this capacity for other-regard, though, they found to be reflectiveness. Jody D. Nyquist and Jo Sprague emphasize the importance of reflectiveness for the development of teaching professionals. They note that while TAs might reach a certain functional level of competence without being very reflective, they will undoubtedly "hit a ceiling of 'mere competence' if it is not accompanied with increasingly sophisticated reflection on teaching," such as on their own strengths and weaknesses as teachers.[13] To encourage the development of reflectiveness, Nyquist and Sprague find that it helps for TAs to be involved in reflective conversation with the professors who are supervising them when those professors are themselves reflective as teachers. Through such reflective conversation these supervisors are able to model reflectivity, assist the TA with developing the language for reflection and promote the TA's reflective process by asking reflective questions.

A similar dynamic, I have observed, occurs for us as we are formed to be ministering professionals. Initially, ministerial interns beginning to serve in a place of ministry tend to be very concerned with their own acceptance in the congregation and with their sense of competence in the arts of ministry. It is not hyperbole to say they are worried about their worthiness in the position—both in terms of their job performance and their acceptance by others.

Anxiety at several levels can mark students' experience, especially in the initial period of encounter. They might be anxious about their abilities and competence with tasks of ministry. They can experience anxiety over their acceptance by others. Students pursuing ordination can experience high levels of anxiety about confirming their call to ministry, and they can

---

12. Wulff et al., "Development of Graduate Students as Teaching Scholars," 60–61; see also Austin, "Development of Graduate Students as Prospective Teaching Scholars."

13. Nyquist and Sprague, "Thinking Developmentally about TAs," 82.

worry about their putative foibles becoming visible to denominational judicatories. Such anxieties can interfere not only with students' abilities for empathy, solidarity, and social role-taking; it also can interfere with their reflectiveness. It is largely because of the importance of these dynamics, pertaining to acceptance during the initial phase of entering a ministry, that we focused on aspects of entering and transition in ministry in chapters 2 and 3.

As these internships progress, though, ministerial interns typically find themselves increasingly accepted by others even as they find themselves successfully accomplishing various tasks of ministry such as preaching. As they become more comfortable in their pastoral roles—with regard to both job performance and social interaction—they become less self-concerned and more genuinely focused on their parishioners and supervisors alike as fellow companions in religious life and service. This fellow feeling, though, this other-regard is an acquired capacity. It is a relatively high level of skill predicated on having addressed legitimate issues of self-concern at an earlier stage. The anxieties relative to earlier issues of self-worthiness tend to preclude the full development of this capacity to focus on others. Once those anxieties about self-acceptance and competence are assuaged, the intern is freed to focus with greater authenticity on parishioners and supervisors alike as fellow servants.

Reflectiveness is key for continued professional development—whether for teachers or ministers. The process of encouraging greater reflectiveness among TAs described above also has parallels with the development of reflectiveness among those of us preparing for ministry. We can benefit from the modeling of mentors—not just with regard to learning the tasks of ministry, but with regard to the reflective process itself. The development of the skill of reflection will allow ministerial students to attend not just to the tasks at hand but to the larger tasks of learning new skills, acquiring increasing competence, facing new challenges, starting projects, and working with others in increasingly deep appreciation for them.

Praxeological education for ministry, such as programs in theological field education, can best take advantage of engagement with others in shared practice to the degree that reflectivity is nurtured. Several strategies help to encourage such reflectivity. First, volition for participating in such programs increases student openness to new community and to the influences that community might have in shaping students as persons and as pastors. Simply, the more choice we have in beginning a situation of ministry with others, the more open we are to learning about ourselves in the context of those relationships. Similarly, second, the degree to which we can pace our encounters and engagements with others also helps us to be more open and to avoid inner defensiveness. This self-directed pace is facilitated by being able to make use of such means as crafting one's own learning goals and the timetables associated with them. Third, repetitive use of the cyclical method of practical theology allows for incremental and cumulative advances of insight. Even if authentic social solidarity is elusive from the outset, the repetitive nature of the cyclical method allows for learning to build and reflection to deepen over time.[14] Fourth, the duration of experiences such as internships and cross-cultural encounters is an important factor to take into account. While a series of shorter cultural immersions can keep a learning curve steep, it can also keep defensiveness alert because of the many rapid encounters. Internships of longer duration allow us to work through initial areas of anxiety, to establish more authentic solidarity with others, and to develop the cultural capital for deepening involvement. Fourth and finally, reflective skill is best encouraged if engaged and modeled by supervisors, teachers, and peers in both the ministry context and the classroom.

Reflectivity is key for progressing to increasing levels of competence and authentic engagement with others. Practical theology is, after all, about theological reflection on practice—for ourselves as practitioners in ministry, for ourselves as a ministering community, and for ourselves in the ever-widening world of which we are a part.

Conclusion

We have come full circle. In chapter 1, we began by reflecting on ourselves as individuals with social location and as persons belonging within community. In chapters 2 and 3, we further reflected on the ambiguous nature of pastors as both cultural insiders and outsiders in their own congregations. In chapter 4 we attended to action-reflection theory in developing skill as reflective practitioners in ministry. In chapter 5, we noticed that organizational theory had been shaped by an appreciation of organizations as cultures, and we looked further at some of the ways congregations can be

---

14. Don Browning emphasized this point with me in personal conversation at the Biennial Meeting of the International Academy of Practical Theology, Chicago, July 30—August 3, 2009.

seen as cultures. Later chapters of this book have attended to the relevance of a wider public for us both as theologians and as practitioners in the life of faith. The cyclical method we have employed has allowed us to notice the relation between specifically Christian practices and wider practice as the web of social relations. It has allowed us to bridge critically between our theological reflection and our analysis of ideologies and social forces impinging on us. This broadening of our theological attention to encompass the possibilities and problems of the larger social world has now led us back to affirm the importance of our own self-reflection as people practicing ministry in community.

Exercise for Reflection

Many of the exercises in this book have invited readers to reflect on his or her own social context and practice of ministry. We have utilized a conceptual grid and a cyclical method to aid us in these reflections. Beginning with our own social location, we have tended to move in a clockwise direction around through successive quadrants in our grid. You may want to look back now over those earlier exercises for reflection and notice the movement of your own thought.

To use Holland and Henriot's language, we have begun with "insertion" in a local community, proceeded to "social analysis" of that community, and engaged in "theological reflection" in conversation with our emerging understanding of that community. At each point, we have looked for bridges and connections (as well as contradictions) between each of these quadrants as we have proceeded. The next movement in Holland and Henriot's method would lead to "pastoral planning." This is represented by the lower-right quadrant on our methodological grid. This quadrant pertains to our practice of Christian ministry—not just as individual practitioners but also as congregated together in fellowship or organized together in service. Looking back on your reflections up to this point, what seem to be the implications for your own "pastoral planning"—for your own ministry in concerted effort with others? Perhaps fill in that lower-right quadrant of the grid afresh with your thoughts about ministry. What are you discerning about your Christian practice in church and society? What is your next step?

Bibliography

Ammerman, Nancy Tatom. *Congregation & Community*. New Brunswick, NJ: Rutgers University Press, 2001.
Ammerman, Nancy T. et al., eds. *Studying Congregations: A New Handbook*. Nashville: Abingdon, 1998.
Argyris, Chris. *Overcoming Organizational Defenses: Facilitating Organizational Learning*. Boston : Allyn and Bacon, 1990.
Argyris, Chris, and Donald A. Schön. *Theory in Practice: Increasing Professional Effectiveness*. San Francisco: Jossey-Bass, 1974.
Aronson, Elliot. *The Social Animal*. Series of Books in Psychology. San Francisco: Freeman, 1976.
Asad, Talal, ed. *Anthropology & the Colonial Encounter*. London: Ithaca, 1973.
Austin, Ann. "The Development of Graduate Students as Prospective Teaching Scholars." Panel presentation for Conference on National Surveys and Studies on Doctoral Education,14 April 2000. http://depts.washington.edu/envision/project_resources/2000_conf_pages/2000_panel_surveys.html#Austin/.
Bass, Dorothy C. *Practicing Our Faith*. San Francisco: Jossey-Bass, 1997.
Bass, Dorothy C., and Craig Dykstra, eds. *For Life Abundant: Practical Theology, Theological Education, and Christian Ministry*. Grand Rapids: Eerdmans, 2008.
Bateson, Gregory. "A Theory of Play and Phantasy." In *Steps to an Ecology of Mind*. New York: Ballentine, 1972. First published in *Psychiatric Research Reports* 2 (Dec. 1955) 39–51.
Bolman, Lee G., and Terrence E. Deal. *Reframing Organizations: Artistry, Choice, and Leadership*. 2nd ed. Jossey-Bass Business & Management Series. San Francisco: Jossey-Bass, 1997.
Browning, Don S. *A Fundamental Practical Theology: Descriptive and Strategic Proposals*. Minneapolis: Fortress, 1996.
———, ed. *Practical Theology: The Emerging Field in Theology, Church, and World*. San Francisco: Harper & Row, 1983.
Bush, Joseph E., Jr. *Gentle Shepherding: Pastoral Ethics and Leadership*. St. Louis: Chalice, 2006.
Bush, Joseph E., and Sue Withers. "Which Religion is Better?" In *Brimming with God: Reflecting Theologically on Cases in Ministry*, edited by Barbara J. Blodgett and Matthew Floding, 133–46. Eugene, OR: Pickwick Publications, 2015.
Carroll, Jackson W. *As One with Authority: Reflective Leadership in Ministry*. Louisville: Westminster John Knox, 1991.

Bibliography

———. "Leadership and the Study of the Congregation." In *Studying Congregations: A New Handbook,* edited by Nancy T. Ammerman et al., 167–95. Nashville: Abingdon, 1998.

Carroll, Jackson W. et al., eds. *Handbook for Congregational Studies.* Nashville: Abingdon, 1986.

Carroll, Lee. "The Forming Work of Congregations." In *Welcome to Theological Field Education!,* edited by Matthew Floding, 79–89. Herndon, VA: Alban Institute, 2011.

Chopp, Rebecca S. "Practical Theology and Liberation." In *Formation and Reflection: The Promise of Practical Theology,* edited by Lewis S. Mudge and James N. Poling, 120–38. Philadelphia: Fortress, 1987.

Cooper-White, Pamela. *Braided Selves: Collected Essays on Multiplicity, God, and Persons.* Eugene, OR: Cascade Books, 2011.

Crane, Julia G., and Michael V. Angrosino. *Field Projects in Anthropology: A Student Handbook.* Long Grove, IL: Waveland, 1992.

DiMaggio, Paul J. *The Relevance of Organization Theory to the Study of Religion.* PONPO Working Paper No. 174 and ISPS Working Paper No. 2174. New Haven: Program on Non-Profit Organizations and Institution for Social and Policy Studies at Yale University, 1992.

Dudley, Carl S. *Community Ministry: New Challenges, Proven Steps to Faith-Based Initiatives* Bethesda, MD: Alban Institute, 2002.

Dudley, Carl S., and Nancy T. Ammerman. *Congregations in Transition: A Guide for Analyzing, Assessing, and Adapting in Changing Communities.* San Francisco: Jossey-Bass, 2002.

Dyck, Arthur. *On Human Care: An Introduction to Ethics.* Nashville: Abingdon, 1977.

Eagleton, Terry. *The Idea of Culture.* Blackwell Manifestos. Malden, MA.: Blackwell, 2000.

Farber-Robertson, Anita. *Learning While Leading: Increasing Your Effectiveness in Ministry.* Bethesda, MD: Alban Institute, 2000.

Farley, Edward. "Interpreting Situations: An Inquiry into the Nature of Practical Theology." In *Formation and Reflection: The Promise of Practical Theology,* edited by Lewis S. Mudge and James N. Poling, 1–26. Philadelphia: Fortress, 1987.

———. "Theology and Practice Outside the Clerical Paradigm." In *Practical Theology: The Emerging Field in Theology, Church, and World,* edited by Don S. Browning, 21–41. San Francisco: Harper & Row, 1983.

Festinger, Leon. "Cognitive Dissonance." In *Readings about the Social Animal,* edited by Elliot Aronson, 99–113. San Francisco: Freeman, 1973. First published in *Scientific American* 107/4 (1962).

Foster, Charles R. *Embracing Diversity: Leadership in Multicultural Congregations.* Bethesda, MD: Alban Institute, 1997.

Fowler, James W. "Practical Theology and Theological Education: Some Models and Questions." *Theology Today* 42 (1985) 43–58.

Frankena, W. K. "Ethics and the Environment." In *Ethics and Problems of the 21st Century,* edited by K. E. Goodpaster and K. M. Sayer, 3–20. Notre Dame: University of Notre Dame Press, 1979.

Francis I, Pope. *Laudato Sí.* Encyclical Letter of The Holy Father Francis on Care for Our Common Home. Vatican Web site. 15 January 2016. http://w2.vatican.va/content/francesco/en/encyclicals/documents/papa-francesco_20150524_enciclica-laudato-si.html/.

Bibliography

Freire, Paulo. *Pedagogy of the Oppressed*. Translated by Myra Berman Ramos. New York: Continuum, 1993.
Gadamer, Hans-Georg. *Truth and Method*. New York: Crossroad, 1982.
Gardner, Howard. *Developmental Psychology: An Introduction*. Boston: Little, Brown, 1978.
Geertz, Clifford. *The Interpretation of Cultures*. New York: Basic Books, 1973.
Gennep, Arnold van. *The Rites of Passage*. Translated by Monika B. Vizedom and Gabrielle L. Caffee. Chicago: University of Chicago Press, 1960 (French ed., 1909).
Goffman, Erving. *Frame Analysis: An Essay on the Organization of Experience*. Cambridge: Harvard University Press, 1974.
Green, Laurie. *Let's Do Theology: A Pastoral Cycle Resource Book*. London: Continuum, 1990.
———. *Let's Do Theology: Resources for Contextual Theology*. London: Mowbray, 2009.
———. "Why Do Theological Reflection?" In *Urban Theology: A Reader*, edited by Michael Northcott, 11–18. London: Cassell, 1998.
Grierson, Denham. *Transforming a People of God*. Melbourne: Joint Board of Christian Education of Australia and New Zealand, 1984.
Groome, Thomas H. *Christian Religious Education: Sharing Our Story and Vision*. San Francisco: Harper & Row, 1980.
———. *Sharing Faith: A Comprehensive Approach to Religious Education and Pastoral Ministry: The Way of Shared Praxis*. San Francisco: HarperSanFrancisco, 1991.
Gutierrez, Gustavo. *The Power of the Poor in History: Selected Writings*. Translated by Robert R. Barr. Maryknoll: Orbis, 1983.
Hastings, Thomas John. *Practical Theology and the One Body of Christ: Toward a Missional-Ecumenical Model*. Grand Rapids: Eerdmans, 2007.
Heinz, Donald. "The Sabbath in Fiji as Guerrilla Theatre." *Journal of the American Academy of Religion* 61 (1993) 415–42.
Hillman, George M., Jr. *Ministry Greenhouse: Cultivating Environments for Practical Learning*. Herndon, VA: Alban Institute, 2008.
Hirsh, Alan. *The Forgotten Ways: Reactivating the Missional Church*. Grand Rapids: Brazos, 2006.
Hirsh, Alan, with Darryn Altclass. *The Forgotten Ways Handbook: A Practical Guide for Developing Missional Churches*. Grand Rapids: Brazos, 2009.
Holland, Joe, and Peter Henriot, SJ. *Social Analysis: Linking Faith and Justice*. Rev. ed. Maryknoll, NY: Orbis, 1983.
Josselson, Ruthellen. "The Hermeneutics of Faith and the Hermeneutics of Suspicion." *Narrative Inquiry* 14 (2004) 3. http://ruthellenjosselson.com/articles/josselson.ni.14-1.1e.pdf/.
Kirk, J. Andrew. *What Is Mission? Theological Explorations*. Minneapolis: Fortress, 2000.
Kluckhohn, Clyde. *Mirror for Man: The Relation of Anthropology to Modern Life*. New York: McGraw-Hill, 1949.
Kretzmann, John P., and John L. McKnight. *Building Communities from the Inside Out: A Path toward Finding and Mobilizing a Community's Assets*. Evanston, IL: The Asset-Based Community Development Institute, Institute for Policy Research, Northwestern University, distributed by ACTA Publications, 1993.
Lamb, Matthew. *Solidarity with Victims: Toward a Theology of Social Transformation*. New York: Crossroad, 1982.

Bibliography

Lee, Jung Young. *Marginality: The Key to Multicultural Theology*. Minneapolis: Fortress, 1995.

Liedke, Gerhard. "Solidarity in Conflict." In *Faith and Science in an Unjust World: Report of the World Council of Churches' Conference on Faith, Science and the Future, Massachusetts Institute of Technology, Cambridge, USA, 12-24 July 1979*. Vol. 1, *Plenary Presentations*, edited by Roger L. Shinn, 73–80. Geneva: World Council of Churches, 1980.

Loetscher, Catherine. "The Use of a Distinction between Moral Agent, Moral Patient and Object. Some Remarks." *Global Bioethics: problemi di bioetica* 15/3 (2002) 21–25. http://eprints.unifi.it/archive/00000995/01/03_Loetscher.pdf/.

Luzbetak, Luis J. *The Church and Cultures: New Perspectives in Missiological Anthropology*. American Society of Missiology 12. Maryknoll, NY: Orbis, 1988.

Macleod, Duncan. "Action Science and Theological Reflection in Community." http://www.postkiwi.com/2004/learning-community/.

Maffley-Kipp, Laurie F. et al., eds. *Practicing Protestants: Histories of Christian Life in America, 1630–1965*. Baltimore: Johns Hopkins University Press, 2006.

Mannheim, Karl. *Ideology and Utopia: An Introduction to the Sociology of Knowledge*. Translated by Louis Wirth and Edward Shils. New York: Harvest, 1936.

Massey, Floyd, Jr., and Samuel Berry McKinney. *Church Administration in the Black Perspective*. Rev. ed. Valley Forge, PA: Judson, 2003.

Mathews, Rosita deAnn. "Using Power from the Periphery: An Alternative Theological Model for Survival in Systems." In *A Troubling in My Soul: Womanist Perspectives on Evil and Suffering*, edited by Emile M. Townes, 92–106. The Bishop Henry McNeal Turner Studies in North American Black Religion 8. Maryknoll, NY: Orbis, 2005.

McLeod, John. *Qualitative Research in Counselling and Psychotherapy*. Thousand Oaks, CA: Sage, 2001.

Míguez Bonino, José. *Toward a Christian Political Ethics*. Philadelphia: Fortress, 1983.

Mudge, Lewis S., and James N. Poling, eds. *Formation and Reflection: The Promise of Practical Theology*. Philadelphia: Fortress, 1987.

Niebuhr, H. Richard. *The Responsible Self*. San Francisco: Harper & Row, 1963.

Noonan, William R. *Discussing the Undiscussable: A Guide to Overcoming Defensive Routines in the Workplace*. San Francisco: Jossey-Bass/Wiley, 2007.

Nouwen, Henri J. M. *The Dance of Life: Weaving Sorrows and Blessings into One Joyful Step*. Edited by Michael Andrew Ford. Notre Dame: Ave Maria, 2005.

———. *Reaching Out: The Three Movements of the Spiritual Life*. Garden City, NY: Image, 1986.

Nyquist, Jody D., and Jo Sprague. "Thinking Developmentally about TAs." In *The Professional Development of Graduate Teaching Assistants*, edited by Michele Marincovich et al., 61–88. Bolton, MA: Anker, 1998.

Ogletree, Thomas W. *The World Calling: The Church's Witness in Politics and Society*. Louisville: Westminster John Knox, 2004.

O'Reilly, Karen. *Ethnographic Methods*. London: Routledge, 2005.

Osmer, Richard R. *Practical Theology: An Introduction*. Grand Rapids, Eerdmans, 2008.

Parsons, George, and Speed B. Leas. *Understanding Your Congregation as a System: The Manual*. 2 vols. Bethesda, MD: Alban Institute, 1993.

Piaget, Jean. *Six Psychological Studies*. Translated by Anita Tenzer and David Elkind. New York: Random House, 1967.

Bibliography

Ramsbotham, Oliver, et al. *Contemporary Conflict Resolution*. Cambridge, UK: Polity, 2005. http://www.polity.co.uk/ccr/contents/.

Richardson, Ronald W. *Creating a Healthier Church: Family Systems, Leadership, and Congregational Life*. Creative Pastoral Care and Counseling Series. Minneapolis: Fortress, 1996.

Ricoeur, Paul. "The Conflict of Interpretations: Debate with Hans-Georg Gadamer." In *A Ricoeur Reader: Reflection and Imagination*, edited by Mario J. Valdés, 216–41. Theory/Culture Series 2. Toronto: University of Toronto Press, 1991.

———. *Freud and Philosophy: An Essay on Interpretation*. The Dwight Harrington Terry Foundation Lectures on Religion in the Light of Science and Philosophy. Translated by Denis Savage. New Haven: Yale University Press, 1970.

Roxburgh, Alan J. *The Missionary Congregation, Leadership & Liminality*. Christian Mission and Modern Culture. Harrisburg, PA: Trinity, 1997.

———. *The Sky is Falling: Leaders Lost in Transition*. Eagle, ID: ACI, 2005.

Schön, Donald A. *The Reflective Practitioner: How Professionals Think in Action*. New York: Basic, 1983.

Scheff, Thomas. *Goffman Unbound! A New Paradigm for Social Science*. Advancing the Sociological Imagination. Boulder: Paradigm, 2006.

Schleiermacher, Friedrich. *Brief Outline on the Study of Theology*. Translated by Terrence N. Tice. Richmond: John Knox, 1966 (German eds., 1811, 1830).

Schreiter, Robert J. *Constructing Local Theologies*. Maryknoll, NY: Orbis, 1985.

———. "Theology in the Congregation: Discovering and Doing." In *Studying Congregations: A New Handbook*, edited by Nancy T. Ammerman, et al., 23–39. Nashville: Abingdon, 1998.

Segundo, Juan Luis, SJ. *The Liberation of Theology*. Translated by John Drury. 1979. Reprinted, Eugene, OR: Wipf & Stock, 2002.

Smith, Philip. *Cultural Theory: An Introduction*. 21st-Century Sociology. Malden, MA: Blackwell, 2004.

Snow, Luther K. *The Power of Asset Mapping: How Your Congregation Can Act on Its Gifts*. Herndon, VA: Alban Institute, 2004.

Steier, Frederick. "Research as Self-Reflexivity, Self-Reflexivity as Social Process." In *Research and Reflexivity*, edited by Frederick Steier, 1–11. London: Sage, 1991.

Swinton, John, and Harriet Mowat. *Practical Theology and Qualitative Research*. London: SCM, 2006.

Tanner, Kathryn. *Theories of Culture: A New Agenda for Theology*. Guides to Theological Inquiry. Minneapolis: Fortress, 1997.

Tappan, M. "Analyzing Stories of Moral Experience: Narrative, Voice, and the Dialogical Self." *Journal of Narrative and Life History* 7 (1997) 379–86.

Thompson, George B., Jr. *How to Get along with Your Church: Creating Cultural Capital for Doing Ministry*. Cleveland: Pilgrim, 2001.

Tracy, David. *The Analogical Imagination: Christian Theology and the Culture of Pluralism*. New York: Crossroad, 1981.

———. *Blessed Rage for Order: The New Pluralism in Theology*. Minneapolis: Winston Seabury, 1975.

———. "The Foundations of Practical Theology." In *Practical Theology: The Emerging Field in Theology, Church, and World*, edited by Don S. Browning, 61–82. San Francisco: Harper & Row, 1983.

Troeltsch, Ernst. *The Social Teaching of the Christian Churches*. 2 vols. Translated by Olive Wyon. New York: Macmillan, 1931 (German ed., 1911).

Trumbauer, Jean Morris. *Created and Called: Discovering Our Gifts for Abundant Living*. Minneapolis: Augsburg Fortress, 1999.

———. *Sharing the Ministry: A Practical Guide for Transforming Volunteers into Ministry*. Minneapolis: Augsburg, 1995.

Turner, Victor. *Dramas, Fields, and Metaphors: Symbolic Action in Human Society*. Symbol, Myth, and Ritual. Ithaca: Cornell University Press, 1974.

———. *The Ritual Process: Structure and Anti-Structure*. Ithaca: Cornell University Press, 1969.

Tuwere, Ilaitia S. *Vanua: towards a Fijian Theology of Place*. Suva, Fiji: Institute of Pacific Studies, 2002.

Veling, Terry A. *Practical Theology: On Earth as It Is in Heaven*. Maryknoll, NY: Orbis, 2005.

Ward, Jeffrey J., and Oswald Werner. "Difference and Dissonance in Ethnographic Data." *Communication and Cognition* 17 (1984) 219–43.

Warnock, G. J. *The Object of Morality*. London: Methuen, 1971.

Waterman, Robert. *What America Does Right: Learning from Companies that Put People First*. New York: Norton, 1994.

Watzlawick, Paul et al. *Change: Principles of Problem Formation and Problem Resolution*. New York: Norton, 1974.

Weber, Max. *The Protestant Ethic and the Spirit of Capitalism*. Translated by Talcott Parsons. New York: Scribner, 1958 (German ed., 1904–5).

Werner, Oswald, and G. Mark Schoepfle. *Systematic Fieldwork*. Vol. 1, *Foundations of Ethnography and Interviewing*. Newbury Park, CA: Sage, 1987.

Wilcox, Mary M. *Developmental Journey: A Guide to the Development of Logical and Moral Reasoning and Social Perspective*. Nashville: Abingdon, 1979.

Williams, Raymond. *Keywords: A Vocabulary of Culture and Society*. 1st ed. New York: Oxford University Press, 1976.

———. *Keywords: A Vocabulary of Culture and Society*. Rev. ed. New York: Oxford University Press, 1983.

Willig, Carla. *Qualitative Research in Psychology: A Practical Guide to Theory and Method*. Buckingham: Open University Press, 2001.

Winquist, Charles E. *Practical Hermeneutics: A Revised Agenda for the Ministry*. Scholars Press Study Aids 1. Missoula, MT: Scholars, 1979.

Wulff, Donald H. et al. "The Development of Graduate Students as Teaching Scholars: A Four-Year Longitudinal Study." In *Paths to the Professoriate: Strategies for Enriching the Preparation of Future Faculty*, 46–73. Jossey-Bass Higher and Adult Education Series. San Francisco: Jossey-Bass, 2004.

Index

acculturation, 29
adaptive, 23, 38, 69
administration, x, xiii, 54, 65–66
agent, agency, 7–9, 11, 13, 15, 45, 52, 79, 112, 155, 158, 161–62
Altclass, Darryn, 34, 177
Andrews, Dale, xiv
Angrosino, Michael, 19, 21–22, 176
anxiety, 82, 86, 170–72
Argyris, Chris, xiii, 53, 57, 60, 63, 175
Aronson, Elliot, 61, 175, 176
Asad, Talal, 162, 175
asset mapping, 83–84, 110–12
Asset-Based Community Development Institute, 83, 111, 177
assets, 80–83, 87–88, 96, 110–12
Association of Practical Theology, 135–36
Austin, Ann, 170, 175
authority, authorize, 22–24, 31–39, 42–43, 49–50, 51, 66, 76–77, 79, 86, 96

Bass, Dorothy C., 149, 175
Bolman, Lee G., 54, 71–73, 75–81, 85, 175
Bread for the World, 125–26
bridge, bridge notions, bridge practices, 16, 25, 27, 77, 101, 106, 109–14, 120–23, 131, 141, 144–45, 160, 173
Browning, Don S., xiv, 135–43, 146, 148, 155, 168, 172, 175, 176, 179
Bush, Joseph E., Jr., x, 37, 131, 175

calling, x, 76, 84. *See also* vocation.
Carroll, Jackson W., xiii, 36–37, 53–54, 64, 69, 84, 175–76
Carroll, Lee, 85, 176
case for discussion, case for reflection, 10–12, 13–14, 39–42, 65–67
Chopp, Rebecca S., 147–48, 150–51, 176
classism, 8, 105
clinical pastoral education, 46, 163
cognitive dissonance, 61–63, 67
communitas, 32–34
Cone, James, xii
congregational studies, xi, xiii, xiv, 71, 80
conscientization, 52
contextual studies, xi, 166
contradiction, xi, 50, 51–53, 62, 64, 68, 103, 110–11, 173
Cooper-White, Pamela, 44, 56, 176
Couture, Pamela, xiv
Crane, Julia, 19, 176
critical correlation, 143–44, 146–47, 155, 160
culture shock, 19, 30
culture, definition, 18

Deal, Terrence E., 54, 71–73, 75–81, 85, 175
decision-making ethics, x, 6–7, 12
dilemma, 12–13, 161
DiMaggio, Paul J., 70–71, 85, 176
Dudley, Carl S., 84, 176
Dyck, Arthur, 7, 176
Dykstra, Craig, 149, 175

Index

Eagleton, Terry, 18, 176
ecology, ecological, x, 3, 71, 80–81, 84–88, 108–9, 112, 116, 118–20
enculturation, enculturated, 29, 158, 162
epistemology, epistemological, 21, 81, 151, 163, 165, 168–69
espoused theory, 50, 60–61, 67
ethics x-xi, 5–8, 15, 54, 127–31, 135
exercise for reflection, 21–22, 26–28, 49, 68, 85–89, 101–3, 122, 129–30, 133, 144–45, 156, 173

family systems, 82–83
Farber-Robertson, Anita, xiii, 57–61, 63–64, 68, 69, 152, 176
Farley, Edward, 136–37, 140–41, 168, 176
Festinger, Leon, 61–62, 176
field education, ix, xi-xiv, 163, 165–67, 171
Fiji, xii, xv, 24–25, 27, 30, 35, 117–19
Fisch, Richard, 56
Foster, Charles R., 38, 176
Fowler, James W., 146–48, 151, 176
frames, framing, reframing, xiii, 6, 17, 43–44, 53–56, 59–60, 62, 64, 66–68, 69–89, 93–94, 108, 112, 125, 162
Frankena, W. K., 8, 176
Freire, Paulo, 51–53, 132, 138, 177
Freud, Sigmund, 152, 154, 179

Gadamer, Hans-Georg, 142, 177, 179
Gardner, Howard, 61, 177
Geertz, Clifford, 78, 159, 177
Gennep, Arnold van, 31, 177
global warming, 118
God, 3, 23, 29, 33, 37, 44, 55, 76, 84, 94, 96, 97, 113, 117–20, 127, 130, 149, 158
God's Pacific People, 120
Goffman, Erving, 54, 71, 177, 179
Green, Laurie, xiii, 132–34, 143–45, 160, 168, 177
greenhouse, 118, 120
Grierson, Denham, xii, 177

Groome, Thomas H., xiv, 136–40, 142–44, 168, 177
Gutierrez, Gustavo, 147, 177

Henriot, Peter, xii, 107, 109, 111, 124, 130, 132–34, 137, 164, 168, 173, 177
hermeneutic, hermeneutical, xi, 46–49, 53, 81, 99, 104, 128, 131, 133, 136, 137–40, 142–44, 147, 151–56, 158, 162
heterosexism, 8
Hirsh, Alan, 33–34, 177
Holland, Joe, xii, 107, 109, 111, 124, 130, 132–34, 137, 164, 168, 173, 177
hospitality, 21, 24–28, 29

immigration, 14, 105
inculturation, 29, 114
intern, internship, ix, xii, xv, 19, 22–23, 30, 36, 50, 58, 61–62, 67, 165–68, 170–72
International Academy of Practical Theology, 135, 172
irony, ironic, 15, 18, 23, 42, 51, 79, 116, 163, 168–69
islands, xii, 117–20

Josselson, Ruthellen, 154–55, 177

Keely, Barbara Anne, 166
Kirk, J. Andrew, 114, 177
Kluckhohn, Clyde, 20, 177
Kretzmann, John P., 83–84, 88, 110–12, 177

ladder of inference, 63, 67, 152–53
Lamb, Matthew, 147–48, 177

leadership, x, xiii, 8, 14, 17, 23, 25, 29–34, 38–39, 50, 51, 53, 57–59, 63–67, 69, 71–72, 77–80, 82–84, 96, 153, 163, 167
Leas, Speed B., 66, 178
Lee, Jung Young, 23, 178
liberation, xi-xii, 15, 29, 81, 99, 124, 127–34, 136–38, 146–48, 150–56, 157, 162, 164–65, 167

182

INDEX

Liedke, Gerhard, 9, 178
liminal, liminality, 20, 29, 31–35, 38–39, 41–45, 49, 153
Loetscher, Catherine, 8, 178
Luzbetak, Louis J., 29, 114, 178

Macleod, Duncan, 67, 178
Maffley-Kipp, Laurie F., 149, 178
Mannheim, Karl, 54, 178
Marx, Karl, 152–54
Massey, Floyd, Jr., 66, 178
matanivanua, 24–25, 27–28, 30
Mathews, Rosita deAnn, 42–44, 178
McKinney, Samuel Berry, 66, 178
McKnight, John L., 83–84, 88, 110–12, 177
McLeod, John, 163, 178
meta-commentary, 60, 64, 68
Míguez Bonino, José, 128–34, 138, 168, 178
missiology, xi–xii, xiv, 29, 33, 114
mission, missional, missionary, x–xi, xv, 16, 32–34, 54–55, 71, 74–75, 86, 89, 112, 114, 117–18, 120, 166–67
moral agent. *See* agent.
moral dilemma. *See* dilemma.
moral patient, 8–9, 13, 15
Mowat, Harriet, 146, 163, 179

Niebuhr, H. Richard, 45, 178
Nietzsche, Friedrich, 152, 154
Noonan, William R., 60, 178
Nouwen, Henri, 29, 178
Nyquist, Jody D., 166, 169–70, 178

O'Reilly, Karen, 162, 178
Oceania, xii, 117–18
Ogletree, Thomas, xii, 4–5, 131, 178
organizational theory, xiii, 85, 172
Osmer, Richard, xiv, 141–43, 148–49, 155, 168, 178

Pacific Theological College, xii, xv, 117–18, 120
Parsons, George, 66, 178
participant observation, 19–20
pastoral authority, 22–24, 33–37, 42, 49–50, 51

pastoral care, x, 22, 42–44, 46, 54–55, 62, 135, 164, 167
performance theory, 77
Piaget, Jean, 61, 178
policy, policies, 6, 166
poverty, xi, 10, 15, 73, 108, 125
praxeological, 4, 114, 138, 151, 157, 163–65, 171
praxis, definitions, 4, 147–49
privilege, xi, 11–12, 15, 36, 45, 147, 151, 153
profession, professional, x, 4–5, 8, 15, 37, 40–42, 52–53, 59, 69, 163, 169–71

racism, 8, 14–15, 105, 109
Ramsbotham, Oliver, 9, 179
reef, 118–20
reflexive, reflexivity, reflectivity, 82, 100, 103, 104, 122, 144, 155–56, 157–72
reframing. *See* frames
Richardson, Ronald W., 82–83, 179
Ricoeur, Paul, 151–55, 158, 179
rites of passage, 31
ritual, ritualize, 19, 24, 27, 31–32, 77–78, 89, 120
Roxburgh, Alan J., 32–34, 179

Sabbath, 119–21
Scheff, Thomas, 54, 179
Schleiermacher, Friedrich, 135, 179
Schmidt, Leigh E., 149
Schön, Donald, xiii, 53–54, 57, 60, 175, 179
Schreiter, Robert J., xii–xiii, 114, 136, 138–40, 160, 179
Segundo, Juan Luis, xi, 131–34, 138, 151, 153, 168, 179
semiology, semiotics, 77, 159
sexism, 8, 14–15, 105
situation, definition 136–37
Snow, Luther K. 83, 110, 179
social location, xv, 6–11, 13–15, 16, 22–23, 36, 81, 95, 100, 103, 105, 110, 153, 156, 158, 162, 164–65, 167, 172–73
society, definition, 3

solidarity, 9–10, 81, 95, 105, 113–14, 120, 124–25, 127–28, 146–48, 150, 154, 165, 167–68, 171–72
Sprague, Jo, 166, 169–70, 178
Steier, Frederick, 162–63, 179
suspicion, xi, 110, 131, 146, 151–56, 158, 162
Swinton, John, 146, 163, 179

Tanner, Kathryn, 161, 179
theory in use, 60–61, 67
thick description, 78
Thompson, George B., Jr., 34–35, 179
Tillich, Paul, 143
Tracy, David, 143, 146, 148, 179
Troeltsch, Ernst, xi-xii, 131, 180
Trumbauer, Jean Morris, 76, 180
Turner, Victor, 31–32, 34, 43–44, 78, 180

Valeri, Mark, 149
Veling, Terry, 18, 180
verbatim, 59–60, 64, 68
vocation, x, 76, 120. *See also* calling.

Ward, Jeffrey J., 20–21, 180
Warnock, G. J., 8, 180
water, 18, 87, 109, 114–20
Watzlawick, Paul, 56, 180
Weakland, John H., 56
Weber, Max, xi, 131, 180
Werner, Oswald, 20–21, 180
Wheeler, Sondra Ely, 166
Wilcox, Mary M., 61, 180
Williams, Raymond, 18, 180
Winquist, Charles E., 46–47, 180
Wulff, Donald H., 170, 180

www.ingramcontent.com/pod-product-compliance
Lightning Source LLC
Chambersburg PA
CBHW031429150426
43191CB00006B/461